PSYCH 101

PSYCHOLOGY *FACTS, BASICS, STATISTICS, TESTS,* AND MORE!

CONTENTS

JEAN PIAGET

ALBERT BANDURA

CARL ROGERS

ABRAHAM MASLOW

THEORIES OF INTELLIGENCE

KURT LEWIN

CARL JUNG

HENRY MURRAY

LEFT AND RIGHT BRAIN

LOVE

KAREN HORNEY

JOHN BOWLBY

ATTRIBUTION THEORY

EMOTION

PERSONALITY

LEADERSHIP THEORIES

DREAMS

ART THERAPY

HYPNOSIS

ALBERT ELLIS

COGNITIVE BEHAVIORAL THERAPY

HEURISTICS

INTRODUCTION: WHAT IS PSYCHOLOGY?

psyche—The Greek word for "spirit, soul, and breath"
logia—The Greek word for "the study of something"

Psychology is the study of mental and behavioral processes. Essentially, those who work in the field of psychology try to give meaning to the questions, "What makes you tick?" and "How do you see the world?" These very simple ideas encompass many different and complicated topics, including emotions, thought processes, dreams, memories, perception, personality, illness, and treatment.

While the roots of psychology date back to the philosophers of Ancient Greece, it wasn't until 1879, when German psychologist Wilhelm Wundt created the first laboratory completely devoted to the study of psychology, that the field really began to take off. Since then, psychology has expanded exponentially into a truly diverse science, often overlapping with other types of scientific studies such as medicine, genetics, sociology, anthropology, linguistics, biology, and even subjects like sports, history, and love.

So put on your thinking cap, make yourself comfortable (perhaps recline on a couch), and prepare to be enlightened; it's time to start learning about yourself in ways you never knew possible. Whether this book is a refresher course or you're learning all of this for the very first time, let's begin. Welcome to *Psych 101*.

IVAN PAVLOV (1849–1936)

The man who studied man's best friend

Ivan Pavlov was born in Ryazan, Russia, on September 14th, 1849. The son of the village priest, Pavlov originally studied theology until 1870, when he abandoned his religious studies and attended the University of St. Petersburg to study physiology and chemistry.

From 1884 to 1886, Pavlov studied under renowned cardiovascular physiologist Carl Ludwig and gastrointestinal physiologist Rudolf Heidenhain. By 1890, Pavlov had become a skilled surgeon and took an interest in the regulation of blood pressure. Without the use of any anesthesia, Pavlov was able to almost painlessly insert a catheter into a dog's femoral artery and record the impact that emotional and pharmacological stimuli had on blood pressure. However, Pavlov's most influential research with dogs—classical conditioning—was yet to come.

From 1890 to 1924, Ivan Pavlov worked at the Imperial Medical Academy as a professor of physiology. In his first ten years at the academy, he began to turn his attention towards the correlation between salivation and digestion. Through a surgical procedure, Pavlov was able to study the gastrointestinal secretions of an animal during its life span within relatively normal conditions; and he conducted experiments to show the relationship between autonomic functions and the nervous system. This research led to the development of Pavlov's most important concept, the conditioned reflex. By 1930, Pavlov had begun using his research on conditioned reflexes to explain human psychoses.

Doctoral Definitions

CONDITIONED REFLEX: A response that becomes associated with a previously unrelated stimulus as a result of pairing the stimulus with another stimulus normally yielding the response.

Though he was praised and supported by the Soviet Union, Pavlov was an outspoken critic of the government's Communist regime and even denounced the government publicly in 1923, following a trip to the United States. When, in 1924, the government expelled the sons of priests at the former Imperial Medical Academy (which was then known as the Military Medical Academy in Leningrad), Pavlov, the son of a priest himself, resigned from his position as professor. Dr. Ivan Pavlov died on February 27th, 1936, in Leningrad.

The Many Accolades of Ivan Pavlov

During his lifetime, the research of Dr. Pavlov was met with great praise.

Here is a sampling of his achievements:

- Elected as a corresponding member of the Russian Academy of Science (1901)
- Awarded a Nobel Prize for Physiology and Medicine (1904)
- Elected Academician of the Russian Academy of Science (1907)
- Awarded honorary doctorate at Cambridge University (1912)
- Received the Order of the Legion of Honour from the Medical Academy of Paris (1915)

CLASSICAL CONDITIONING—LEARNING BY ASSOCIATION

Classical conditioning was Ivan Pavlov's most famous and influential work, and it laid much of the groundwork of behavioral psychology. In essence, the idea of classical conditioning is simply learning something by association. Pavlov identified four basic principles:

1. **The Unconditioned Stimulus:** A stimulus is any act, influence, or agent that creates a response. An unconditioned stimulus is when the stimulus automatically triggers some type of response. For example, if pollen makes a person sneeze, then pollen is an unconditioned stimulus.
2. **The Unconditioned Response:** This is a response that is automatically triggered as a result of the unconditioned stimulus. In essence, this is a natural, unconscious reaction to whatever the stimulus might be. For example, if pollen makes a person sneeze, the sneeze is the unconditioned response.
3. **The Conditioned Stimulus:** When a neutral stimulus (a stimulus that is not related to the

response) becomes associated with an unconditioned stimulus, thus triggering conditioned response.

4. **The Conditioned Response:** This is a response that was learned from the once-neutral stimulus.

Confused? Don't be. It's actually very simple! Imagine if you flinched after hearing a loud sound. The sound triggered a natural response, making it an unconditioned stimulus, and the flinching was the unconditioned response because it was something that you did unconsciously as a result of the unconditioned stimulus.

Now, if you repeatedly witnessed a certain movement happen at the same time as, or a little bit before, the loud noise occurred—for example, a person swinging their fist to slam it on a table—you might then begin to associate that movement with the loud sound, flinching whenever you see a fist move in a similar manner, even if there is no sound. The movement of the fist (the conditioned stimulus) became associated with the unconditioned stimulus (the sound), and made you flinch (the conditioned response).

PAVLOV'S DOGS

Dr. Ivan Pavlov was able to establish these ideas by observing the irregular secretions of nonanesthetized dogs. Pavlov initially began studying digestion in dogs by measuring the amount of saliva that the animals had when both edible and nonedible items were introduced.

Eventually, he began to notice that the dogs would begin salivating every time an assistant entered the room. Believing that the animals were responding to the white coats the assistants wore, Pavlov hypothesized that this production of saliva was actually in response to a certain stimulus, and that these dogs were associating the white coats with the presentation of food. Furthermore, Pavlov noted, the production of saliva that occurred when food was presented to the dogs was an unconditioned reflex, while the production of saliva that was a result of the dogs seeing the white coats was a learned, or conditioned, reflex. To dig deeper into his findings, Pavlov set out to create one of the most famous scientific experiments of all time: Pavlov's dogs.

EXPERIMENT

FOR WHOM THE BELL TOLLS: CONDUCTING THE CONDITIONED RESPONSE EXPERIMENT

BEFORE CONDITIONING

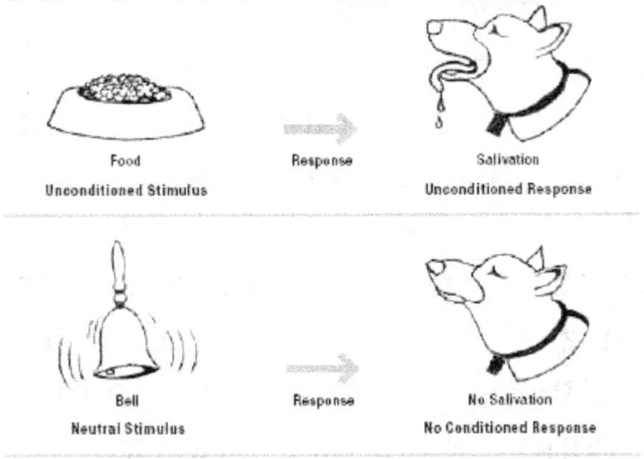

DURING CONDITIONING

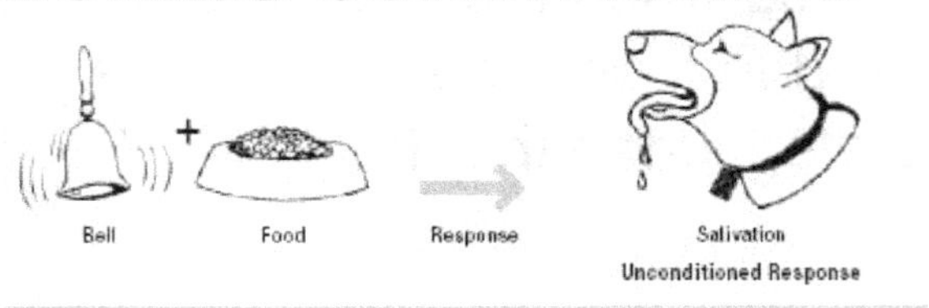

AFTER CONDITIONING

PAVLOV'S DOGS EXPERIMENTAL PROGRESSION

1. The test subjects in this conditioned response experiment are laboratory dogs.
2. First, an unconditioned stimulus must be chosen. In this experiment the unconditioned stimulus is food, which will evoke a natural and automatic response: salivation. For a neutral stimulus, the experiment utilizes the sound of a metronome.
3. Observing the subjects prior to conditioning reveals that saliva is generated when the dogs are exposed to food, and no saliva is generated when the dogs are

exposed to the sound of the metronome.

4. To begin the process, the subjects are repeatedly exposed to the neutral stimulus (the sound of the metronome) and are immediately presented with the unconditioned stimulus (food).
5. Over a period of time, the subjects will begin to equate the sound of the metronome to the delivery of food. The longer the experiment progresses, the more deeply ingrained the conditioning will become.
6. After the conditioning phase is completed, the neutral stimulus (the metronome) will cause the subjects to begin salivating in anticipation of food, regardless of whether or not food is presented. Salivation has become a conditioned response.

Even though he is most well known in popular culture for his famous dogs, the importance of Pavlov's research goes far beyond the production of saliva. His revelations on conditioning and learned responses have played a major role in understanding behavioral modification in humans, and in advancing the treatment of such mental health issues as panic disorders, anxiety disorders, and phobias.

B. F. SKINNER (1904–1990)

It's all about the consequences

Burrhus Frederic Skinner was born on March 20th, 1904, in Susquehanna, Pennsylvania. The son of a lawyer and housewife, Skinner had a warm and stable childhood, and was left with plenty of time for creativity and invention—two traits that would serve him well throughout his career. Having graduated from Hamilton College in 1926, Skinner originally set his sights on becoming a writer. It was while working as a bookstore clerk in New York City that Skinner discovered the works of John B. Watson and Ivan Pavlov, which so fascinated him that he put his plans of becoming a novelist to the side and decided to pursue a career in psychology.

When Skinner was twenty-four years old, he enrolled in the psychology department of Harvard University and began his studies under William Crozier, the chair of the new physiology department. Though not himself a psychologist, Crozier was interested in studying the behavior of animals “as a whole,” an approach that was different than the approaches that psychologists and physiologists took at the time. Instead of trying to figure out all of the processes that were occurring inside the animal, Crozier—and subsequently Skinner—was more interested in the animal’s overall behavior. Crozier’s ideology matched perfectly with the work that Skinner wished to pursue; he was interested in learning how behavior was related to experimental conditions. Skinner’s most significant and influential work, the notion of operant conditioning and the invention of the operant conditioning chamber, came out of his days at Harvard. The work Skinner conducted while at Harvard University is still some of the most important research with regards to behaviorism—work which he taught firsthand to generations of students at his alma mater until he passed away at the age of eighty-six, in 1990.

Celebrating Skinner

B. F. Skinner's work left a profound impact on the world of psychology, and his work did not go unnoticed. Some of his more outstanding citations include:

- President Lyndon B. Johnson awarded Skinner the National Medal of Science (1968)
- Skinner was awarded the Gold Medal of the American Psychological Foundation (1971)
- Skinner was given the Human of the Year Award (1972)
- Skinner received a Citation for Outstanding Lifetime Contribution to Psychology (1990)

OPERANT CONDITIONING AND THE SKINNER BOX

B. F. Skinner's most important work was the concept of operant conditioning. Essentially, operant conditioning is when someone learns a behavior as the result of the rewards and punishments associated with that behavior. Operant conditioning can be broken down into four types:

1. **Positive Reinforcement:** This is when a behavior is strengthened and the probability of it recurring increases because a positive condition was the result.
2. **Negative Reinforcement:** A behavior is strengthened as a result of avoiding or stopping a negative condition.
3. **Punishment:** This occurs when a behavior is weakened and the probability of the behavior recurring decreases due to a negative condition being the result.
4. **Extinction:** When a behavior is weakened because the result did not lead to a positive condition or a negative condition.

Positive and negative reinforcement will strengthen a particular behavior, making it more likely to occur, and punishment and extinction will weaken a particular behavior.

To see operant conditioning in action, B. F. Skinner performed a very simple experiment and invented the operant conditioning chamber, which is now often referred to as the Skinner Box.

EXPERIMENT

THE SKINNER BOX AND OPERANT CONDITIONING

1. To conduct the experiment, begin by placing a hungry rat inside of the box. Every time the rat presses a lever inside the box, it will receive a pellet of food. The rat will soon come to learn that by pressing the lever, it will get food (a positive condition), and thus a behavior is strengthened by positive reinforcement.
2. Next, place a rat into the box and then give it a slight electrical shock (a negative condition) to its feet. If

the rat presses the lever, the shock will stop. Then send another slight electrical shock to the rat's feet. Once again, when the rat presses the lever, the electrical shock stops. Every time the rat is given an electrical shock, the rat learns that in order to stop it, it must press the lever. This is an example of negative reinforcement, because the rat is learning a behavior in order to stop a negative condition.

3. Place a rat into the box and give it a slight electrical shock (the negative condition) on its feet each time it presses the lever. The behavior of pressing the lever will be weakened because of the negative condition: this is an example of punishment.
4. Now, place the rat into the box and do not give it food or an electrical shock whenever the lever is pressed. The rat will not associate a positive or negative condition to the behavior of pressing the lever, and thus this behavior will be

weakened. This is an example of extinction.

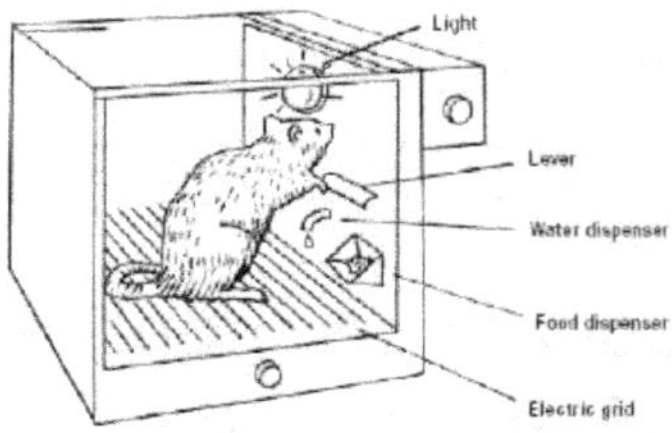

THE SKINNER BOX

The Unfortunate Legacy of the Skinner Box

In 1943, Skinner's pregnant wife asked him to build a safer baby crib for their child. Always the inventor, Skinner created a heated crib that was enclosed with a plexiglass window and called it the Baby Tender. Skinner sent an article to *Ladies' Home Journal*, and they printed the story as "Baby in a Box." With the legacy of Skinner's work in operant conditioning, a rumor spread that Skinner had used his experimental operant conditioning chamber on his own daughter and that it eventually drove her crazy to the point of suicide. These rumors, however, were completely false.

SCHEDULES OF REINFORCEMENT

Another important component of operant conditioning is the notion of schedules of reinforcement. How often and when a behavior is reinforced can greatly affect the strength of the behavior and the rate of response. Positive and negative reinforcement can be used, and the goal is always to strengthen behavior and increase the chances of it happening again. Schedules of reinforcement can be broken down into two types:

1. **Continuous reinforcement:** Every time a behavior occurs, it is reinforced.
2. **Partial reinforcement:** A behavior is reinforced part of the time.

Interestingly, the response that is the result of partial reinforcement is actually more resistant to extinction because these behaviors are learned over time, and not acquired all at once. Partial reinforcement can be further broken down into four schedules:

1. **Fixed-ratio schedules:** After a specific number of responses, the response is reinforced. For example, a rat only gets food pellets after pressing the lever every three times.
2. **Variable-ratio schedules:** Reinforcement occurs after an unpredictable number of responses. For example, a rat presses the lever several times, but a pellet of food is administered at random and is not based on any sort of fixed schedule.
3. **Fixed-interval schedules:** A response is rewarded after an allotted period of time. For example, if a rat presses the lever within a time frame of thirty seconds, it will be given one food pellet. It does not matter how many

times the rat presses the lever, because only one pellet will be given during that time frame.

4. **Variable-interval schedules:** Reinforcement occurs after an unpredictable amount of time. For example, the rat may be rewarded a pellet every fifteen seconds, and then every five seconds, and then every forty-five seconds, etc.

Examples of the four different schedules of reinforcement can be found in everyday life. For instance, a fixed-ratio schedule is commonly found in playing videogames (where the player has to collect a certain number of points or coins to obtain a reward); slot machines exhibit a variable-ratio schedule; having a weekly or biweekly paycheck is an example of a fixed-interval schedule; and when one's boss comes into the office to check on an individual's progress at random times, it is an example of a variable-interval schedule. When learning a behavior that is new, a fixed-ratio schedule is always best, while a variable-interval schedule is extremely resistant to extinction.

Though behaviorism lost its popularity over time, there is no denying the impact of B. F. Skinner. His operant techniques remain vital to mental health professionals in helping treat clients, and his ideas of reinforcement and punishment are still used in teaching and dog training.

SIGMUND FREUD (1856–1939)

The creator of psychoanalysis

Sigmund Freud was born on May 6th, 1856, in Freiberg, Moravia, now the Czech Republic. Freud's mother was his father's second wife, and she was twenty years younger than his father. Freud had two older half-brothers that were around twenty years older than he was; also, he was the first of seven children from his mother. At the age of four, Freud moved from Moravia to Vienna, Austria, where he would spend the majority of his life, despite having claimed to dislike the city.

Freud did well in school, and because he was Jewish—though he later came to identify as an atheist—he attended medical school at the University of Vienna in 1873 (medicine and law were the only viable options available to Jewish men at that time in Vienna). Though Freud wished to pursue neuropsychological research, research positions were extremely hard to come by. As a result, Freud moved into private practice with a focus in neurology.

While training, Freud befriended a physician and psychologist by the name of Josef Breuer. This relationship would prove to be incredibly important to the development of Freud's work once Breuer began treating hysteria patients by using hypnosis and encouraging them to talk about their past. The process of hypnosis, which Breuer's patient Anna O. referred to as "the talking cure," allowed patients to discuss memories that they could not recall during a conscious state; and as a result, the symptoms of their hysteria would be relieved. Freud co-authored *Studies in Hysteria* with Breuer, and then traveled to Paris to learn more about hypnosis under the renowned French neurologist Jean-Martin Charcot.

In 1886, Freud returned to Vienna and began a private practice. Originally, Freud used hypnosis on his neurosis and hysteria patients, but he soon realized that he could get more out of patients by having them sit in a relaxed position (like on a couch) and by encouraging them to say whatever was on their mind (known as free association). By doing so, Freud believed he would be able to analyze what was said and determine what traumatic event in the past was responsible for the patient's current suffering.

Freud's most famous works came in quick succession—in the span of five years, he released three books that would impact psychology for decades to come: 1900's *The Interpretation of Dreams*, in which he introduced the world to the idea of the unconscious mind; 1901's *The Psychopathology of Everyday Life*, where he theorized that slips of the tongue—later known as Freudian slips—were actually meaningful comments revealed by the "dynamic unconscious"; and 1905's *Three Essays on the Theory of Sexuality*, where among other things, he spoke of the now-famous Oedipus complex.

A leading scientific mind of his day, Freud found himself gaining unwanted attention when, in 1933, the Nazi regime came to power in Germany and began burning his works. In 1938, the Nazis seized Austria and Freud had his passport confiscated. It was only due to his international fame and the influence of foreigners that Freud was allowed to move to England, where he remained until his death in 1939.

STAGES OF PSYCHOSEXUAL DEVELOPMENT

Freud's theory of psychosexual development is one of the most well-known and controversial theories in psychology. Freud believed that personality was, for the most part, established by the time a person was six years old and that when a predetermined sequence of stages was successfully completed, it would result in a healthy personality, while failure to do so would lead to an unhealthy personality.

Freud believed that the stages in the sequence were based on erogenous zones (sensitive parts of the body that arouse sexual pleasure, desire, and stimulation) and that failure to complete a stage would make a child fixated on that erogenous zone. This would lead the person to over- or underindulge once he or she was an adult.

Oral Stage (birth–eighteen months)

In this stage, a child focuses on oral pleasures like sucking because they create a sense of comfort and trust. If there is too little or too much gratification in this stage, the child will develop an oral personality or oral fixation and become preoccupied with oral behaviors. According to Freud, people with this type of personality are more likely to bite their nails, smoke, drink, or overeat, and will be gullible, depend on other people, and will always be followers.

Anal Stage (eighteen months–three years)

During this stage, a child's main focus turns towards bladder and bowel control, and a child gains pleasure from controlling these activities. Freud believed that success was achieved in this stage as a result of parents using praise and rewards while toilet training, leaving their child feeling capable and productive—such behavior would lead to the child having a competent, creative personality later on in life. If parents were too lenient to the child during toilet training, he believed, it could lead to an anal-expulsive personality and the child would be destructive, messy, and wasteful. If the parents took an approach that was too strict, or forced toilet training too soon, this could lead to an anal-retentive personality, and the child would develop an obsession with perfection, cleanliness, and control.

Phallic Stage (three–six years)

At this stage, Freud believed the pleasure zones turn towards the genitals, giving rise to one of his most famous ideas, that of the Oedipus complex. Freud believed that, at this stage, a boy unconsciously develops a sexual desire for his mother, sees his father as competition for her affection, and wishes to replace his father. Additionally, the boy will develop castration anxiety as he begins to view his father as someone who is trying to punish him for his Oedipal feelings. Rather than fight with the father, however, the boy will identify with him in an effort to vicariously posses the mother. Fixation at this stage, Freud believed, could lead to sexual deviance and being confused about or having a weak sexual identity.

In 1913, Carl Jung coined the term the "Electra complex," which describes a similar relationship that young girls experience with their fathers. Freud disagreed with this concept, however, believing that girls were actually experiencing penis envy (where resentment and discontent exist because the girls wish that they, themselves, had a penis).

Latency Stage (six years–puberty)

At this stage, sexual urges are suppressed and the sexual energy of the child is directed towards other exchanges like social interactions and intellectual activities. It is during this stage that children play mostly with children of the same sex, and there is no psychosexual development or fixation that occurs.

Genital Stage (puberty–adulthood)

The last stage in Freud's model involves the reawakening of sexual urges and a sexual interest in the opposite sex. If all of the previous stages were completed successfully, the person will be caring and well-balanced, and pleasure will be focused on the genitals. If there is fixation at this stage, the individual may have sexual perversions.

Of course, Freud's theory does have its critics. Freud focused almost exclusively on the development of the male. His research was not based on the behavior of children, but rather on what he was told by his adult patients. Because of the long delay between the hypothetical childhood "cause" and the eventual adulthood "effect" in his theories, it is incredibly difficult to measure or test whether Freud's ideas of psychosexual development are accurate.

STRUCTURAL MODELS OF PERSONALITY

In addition to his conceptions of psychosexual development, Freud believed that there were numerous other driving forces at play that were important to understanding the development of a person's personality. His structural model of personality attempts to describe how the mind works by making distinctions between three parts of personality and the human mind: the id, the ego, and the superego.

Id

Every person is born with an id—the id is responsible for getting the newborn child's basic needs met. Freud claimed that the id is based on something known as a "pleasure principle," which essentially means the id wants whatever feels good at that precise moment and disregards any ramifications. There is no consideration for how the rest of the situation might play out, or for any other people involved. For example, when a baby is hurt, wants something to eat, needs to be changed, or simply wants the attention of others, the id drives the baby to cry until its needs are met.

Ego

The next aspect of the personality—the ego—begins developing naturally over the first three years as a result of the child interacting with the world around him. Because of this, Freud claimed that the ego is based on something he referred to as a "reality principle." The ego comes to realize that there are other people around that also have desires and needs, and that impulsive, selfish behavior can actually lead to harm. The ego has to consider the reality of any particular circumstance while also meeting the needs of the id. For example, when a child thinks twice about doing something inappropriate because he understands the negative outcome that will occur, this is the ego asserting itself.

Superego

The superego develops when a child is five years old and is nearing the end of the phallic stage. This is the part of our personality that is made up of morals and ideals that have been acquired and placed on us by society and our parents. Many people also find the superego to be equivalent to the conscience, since both terms have come to refer to the part of our personality that judges what is right from what is wrong.

Freud believed that, in a truly healthy person, the ego would be stronger than the id and superego so that it could consider the reality of the situation, while both meeting the needs of the id and making sure the superego was not disturbed. In the case of the superego being strongest, a person will be guided by very strict morals, and if the id is strongest, a person will seek pleasure over morality and could end up causing great harm (rape, for example, is when one chooses pleasure-seeking over morality, and is a sign of a strong id).

FREUD'S CONCEPTION OF THE HUMAN PSYCHE

Freud believed that our feelings, beliefs, impulses, and underlying emotions were buried in our unconscious, and therefore not available to the waking mind. However, Freud also believed that there were levels of consciousness beyond just conscious or unconscious. To better understand Freud's theory, imagine an iceberg.

The water surrounding the iceberg is known as the "nonconscious." This is everything that has not become part of our conscious. These are things we have not experienced and are not aware of, and therefore, they do not become part of or shape our personalities in any way.

The tip of the iceberg, our conscious, is only a very small portion of our personality, and since it's the only part of ourselves that we're familiar with, we actually know very little of what makes up our personality. The conscious contains thoughts, perceptions, and everyday cognition.

Directly below the conscious, at the base of the iceberg, is the preconscious or subconscious. If prompted, the preconscious mind can be accessed, but it is not actively part of our conscious and requires a little digging. Things such as childhood memories, our old telephone number, the name of a friend we had when we were younger, and any other deeply stored memories are found in this area. It is in the preconscious mind that the superego can be found.

Since we are only aware of the tip of the iceberg at any given time, the unconscious is incredibly large and consists of those buried, inaccessible layers of our personality. It is here that we find things like fears, immoral urges, shameful experiences, selfish needs, irrational wishes, and unacceptable sexual desires. This is also where the id can be found. The ego is not fixed to one particular part of the iceberg and can be found in the conscious, preconscious, and unconscious.

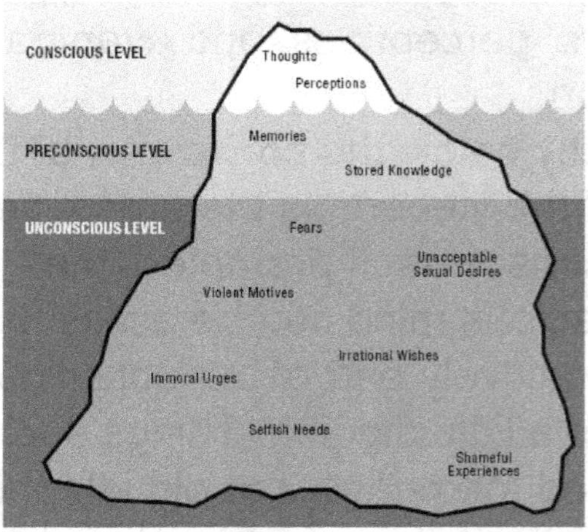

THE ICEBERG METAPHOR

There is no denying just how influential Sigmund Freud was to the fields of psychology and psychiatry. His ideas completely changed the way people viewed personality, sexuality, memory, and therapy, and he is perhaps the most well-known psychologist in the popular vernacular a century after he first arrived as a notable scholar of the mind.

ANNA FREUD (1895–1982)

Think about the kids

Anna Freud was born on December 3rd, 1895, in Vienna, Austria, and was the youngest of Sigmund Freud's six children. Though she felt distant with her siblings and mother, Anna was very close with her father. While she did attend a private school, she claimed to have learned very little in class and that much of her education came from being around her father's friends and associates.

Following high school, Freud began translating her father's work into German and working as an elementary school teacher, where she began to take an interest in child therapy. In 1918, Anna contracted tuberculosis and had to leave her teaching position. During this trying time, she began giving her father accounts of her dreams. As he began to analyze her, Anna quickly cemented her interest in her father's profession and decided to pursue psychoanalysis on her own. Although Anna Freud believed in many of the basic ideas that her father did, she was less interested in the structure of the subconscious and more interested in the ego and the dynamics, or motivations, of one's psyche. This interest led to the publication of her groundbreaking book, *The Ego and Mechanisms of Defense*, in 1936.

Anna Freud is perhaps best known for creating the field of child psychoanalysis, which provided great insight into child psychology; she is also recognized for developing different methods to treat children. In 1923, without ever earning a college degree, Freud began her own children's psychoanalytic practice in Vienna and was named as the chair of the Vienna Psycho-Analytic Society.

In 1938, Anna Freud and her family fled the country and moved to England as a result of the Nazi invasion. In 1941, she founded an institution in London with Dorothy Burlingham and Helen Ross called the Hampstead War Nursery, which served as a foster home and psychoanalytic program for homeless children. Her work with the nursery led to three books: *Young Children in Wartime* in 1942, and both *Infants without Families* and *War and Children* in 1943. In 1945, the nursery closed down and Anna Freud created and served as director of the Hampstead Child Therapy Course and Clinic, a role she maintained until her death. By the time she passed away in 1982, Anna had left a lasting and deep legacy on the field that was possibly only overshadowed by the monumental impact of her father and a handful of other psychologists.

DEFENSE MECHANISMS

To understand Anna Freud's contributions to the notion of defense mechanisms, we must first take a look at the work of her father. Sigmund Freud described certain defense mechanisms the ego uses when dealing with conflicts with the id and superego. He claimed that a reduction of tension is a major drive for most people, and that this tension was largely caused by anxiety. Furthermore, he broke anxiety up into three types:

1. **Reality anxiety:** the fear of real-world events occurring. For example, a person is afraid of being bitten by a dog because they are near a ferocious dog. The easiest way to reduce the tension of reality anxiety is to remove oneself from the situation.
2. **Neurotic anxiety:** the unconscious fear that we will be overpowered by and lose control of the urges of the id, and that this will lead to punishment.
3. **Moral anxiety:** the fear of our moral principles and values being violated, resulting in feelings of shame or guilt. This type of anxiety comes from the superego.

When anxiety occurs, Sigmund Freud claimed that defense mechanisms are used to cope with the anxiety and shield the ego from reality, the id, and the superego. He said that oftentimes these mechanisms unconsciously distort reality and can be overused by a person to avoid a problem. It can therefore be beneficial to understand and uncover these defense mechanisms so that a person may manage their anxiety in a healthier way.

But where does Anna Freud come into play? Most notably, she is responsible for identifying the specific defense mechanisms that the ego uses to reduce tension. They are:

- **Denial:** refusing to admit or recognize that something is occurring or has occurred
- **Displacement:** taking one's feelings and frustrations out on something or someone else that is less threatening
- **Intellectualization:** thinking about something from a cold and objective perspective so that you can avoid focusing on the stressful and emotional part of the situation
- **Projection:** taking your own uncomfortable feelings and attaching them to someone else so it seems as though that person is feeling that way in place of you

- **Rationalization:** while avoiding the actual reason for a feeling or behavior, a person will create credible, but false, justifications
- **Reaction Formation:** behaving in the opposite way to hide one's true feelings
- **Regression:** reverting back to childlike behavior. Anna Freud claimed that a person would act out certain behaviors based on the stage of psychosexual development that they were fixated on. For example, a person stuck in the oral stage might begin to eat or smoke excessively, or become more verbally aggressive
- **Repression:** moving thoughts that make us uncomfortable into our subconscious
- **Sublimation:** converting unacceptable behaviors into a more acceptable form. For example, a person with rage takes up boxing as a way to vent. Sublimation, Freud believed, was a sign of maturity

CHILD PSYCHOANALYSIS

To create a successful therapy for children, Anna Freud originally planned on using her father's work as a guide, so that she could make a timeline and map out a normal rate of growth and development for children. That way, if certain developments, such as hygiene, for example, had been missing or lagging, a therapist could pinpoint the cause to a specific trauma and could then use therapy to address it.

However, Anna quickly came to realize that there were major differences between children and the adult patients her father had seen, and her techniques had to continually change. Whereas Sigmund Freud's patients were self-reliant adults, Anna Freud dealt with children, for whom a major part of their lives involved the presence of their parents. Freud saw the importance of the parents early on; still, a major aspect of child therapy includes parents taking on an active role in the therapy process. For example, parents are generally informed of exactly what goes on during therapy so that they are able to apply the techniques from therapy in everyday life.

Anna Freud also saw the usefulness that child's play could have in therapy. Children could use playing as a means to adapt their reality or confront their problems, and could speak freely during therapy. While play may help a therapist identify a child's trauma and treat it, it doesn't reveal much from the unconscious mind because unlike adults, children have not learned to cover up and repress events and emotions. When a child says something, they mean it!

While she may have begun her career under her father's shadow, Anna Freud proved that she too was an incredibly valuable asset to the world of psychology. Her contributions to her father's work on defense mechanisms and, most importantly, the creation of child psychoanalysis remain extremely important and influential, and a great deal of what we understand about child psychology comes from her work.

LAWRENCE KOHLBERG (1927–1987)

Moral dilemma

Lawrence Kohlberg was born to a wealthy family in Bronxville, New York, on October 25th, 1927. When World War II came around, Kohlberg enlisted as a sailor with the merchant marines—a decision that would prove to have a major impact on him, and subsequently on the field of psychology.

As a sailor, Kohlberg worked on a freighter and helped smuggle Jewish refugees through a British blockade located in Palestine. This would be the first time Kohlberg took an interest in moral reasoning; and, later on in life, he would return to what is now Israel to study more about the moral reasoning of children growing up in kibbutzes (agricultural communities in Israel based on collectivist principles). When he returned from the war, he attended the University of Chicago and studied psychology. Kohlberg scored so highly on his admissions tests that he did not have to take many of the required courses, and he earned his bachelor's degree in psychology in one year. He then earned his PhD in 1958. By 1967, Kohlberg was a professor of education and social psychology at Harvard University, and became widely known and respected with the creation of his theory of the "stages of moral development."

In 1971, Kohlberg was working in Belize when he contracted a parasitic infection. As a result of the disease, Kohlberg spent the next sixteen years of his life battling depression and constant, debilitating pain. On January 19th, 1987, Kohlberg requested a day of leave from the hospital where he was undergoing treatment. After leaving the hospital, Kohlberg drowned himself in Boston Harbor. He was fifty-nine years old.

STAGES OF MORAL DEVELOPMENT

Kohlberg's theory on the stages of moral development was a modification of the work performed by Jean Piaget, the Swiss psychologist. While Piaget described moral development as a two-stage process, Kohlberg identified six stages within three levels. Kohlberg proposed that moral development was a process that continued throughout a person's lifespan. In order to isolate and describe these stages, Kohlberg presented a series of difficult moral dilemmas to groups of young children of different ages. He then interviewed them to find out the reasoning behind each of their decisions, and to see how moral reasoning changed as children grew older.

The Heinz Dilemma

In the Heinz Dilemma, Kohlberg told children a story about a woman in Europe who is near death because she has a special type of cancer. The doctors believe there is one drug that might save her: a form of radium recently discovered by the druggist of that same town. Though it is expensive to make the drug, the druggist is charging ten times what it costs to make. He paid $200 and is charging $2,000 for a small dose. Heinz, the sick woman's husband, tries to borrow money from everyone that he knows but only manages to get $1,000—half of what the druggist is charging. Heinz tells the druggist of his dying wife and asks him if he is willing to sell it at a cheaper price or allow Heinz to pay him back later, but the druggist refuses, saying he discovered the drug and will make money from it. Heinz, desperate, breaks into the druggist's store to steal the drug for his wife. Kohlberg then poses the question, "Should the husband have done that?"

The answers to the dilemmas were not as important to Kohlberg as the reasoning behind the decisions. Based on his research, the children's responses were classified into three levels and six stages.

Level 1: Preconventional Morality

- **Stage 1:** Obedience and Punishment
  In this stage, children view rules as absolutes. Obeying the rules means avoiding punishment. This stage of moral development is particularly common in younger children, though adults can express this reasoning as well.
- **Stage 2:** Individualism and Exchange
  In this stage, children begin to take individual points of view into consideration and judge actions based on how the needs of the individual are served. In the case of the Heinz dilemma, children argued that the choice that best served Heinz's needs was the best course of action.

Level 2: Conventional Morality

- **Stage 3:** Interpersonal Relationships
  In this stage, children focus on living up to expectations set by society or the people close to them. In other words, it is important to be good and nice. For this reason, this is also known as the "good boy–good girl" orientation.
- **Stage 4:** Maintaining Social Order
  At this stage, society as a whole is taken into consideration. This means there is a focus on following the rules to maintain law and order —even in extreme situations— respecting authority, and fulfilling a duty that one has agreed to do.

Level 3: Postconventional Morality

- **Stage 5:** Social Contract and Individual Rights
  In this stage, it becomes understood that people have different beliefs, opinions, and values, and that in order to maintain society, rules of the law should be

based on standards that are agreed upon.

- **Stage 6**: Universal Principles
  The final stage is based on following internal principles of justice and ethics, even if this means going against what the rules and laws state.

It is important to note that Kohlberg believed that it was only possible to pass through these stages in this order and that not every person achieved all of these stages.

CRITICISMS TO THE STAGES OF MORAL DEVELOPMENT

While extremely important and influential, Kohlberg's model has faced criticism. It has been argued that Kohlberg's work reflected a bias towards males (he claimed most men to be at a stage 4 and most women to be at a stage 3), that there is a notable difference between what a person says they ought to do and what they actually end up doing, and that

Kohlberg focused solely on justice but did not take into consideration things like compassion and caring. The way Kohlberg performed his experiment has even been brought into question, due to the fact that he interviewed different children of different ages instead of interviewing the same children over a longer period of time. Regardless, Kohlberg's work in morality remains incredibly influential, and the ideas he set forth are commonly applied to the field of education and are used to understand the behavior of children.

STANLEY MILGRAM

(1933–1984)

A truly shocking psychologist

Stanley Milgram was born on August 13th, 1933, to a Jewish family in New York City. His father was a Hungarian baker and his Romanian mother took over the bakery following his death in 1953. Milgram had always excelled academically and, while attending James Monroe High School, he became active in the school theatre productions. This theatrical experience would prove influential to Milgram, who utilized his background later on in life when creating the realistic experiments he is now most famous for.

In 1953, after graduating from Queens College, New York, with a bachelor's degree in political science, Milgram applied to Harvard University to earn his PhD in social psychology. Though he was initially rejected for having no academic background in psychology, Milgram was finally accepted to Harvard in 1954 and earned his PhD in social psychology in 1960.

In his professional career, Milgram had a strong focus on social issues. From 1959 to 1960, Milgram studied under psychologist Solomon Asch, who was famous for his disturbing experiments on social conformity. In 1961, Milgram would begin his famous obedience study, which remains one of the most infamous and influential psychological experiments ever performed.

In the fall of 1960, Milgram worked as an assistant professor at Yale, and from 1963 to 1966, he was an assistant professor in Harvard's Department of Social Relations. In 1967, Milgram became a lecturer at Harvard; however he was denied tenure, which was likely the result of his controversial Milgram Experiment. That same year, he became a tenured professor at the City University of New York Graduate Center. On December 20th, 1984, Stanley Milgram suffered from a heart attack and died in New York City. He was fifty-one years old.

MILGRAM'S OBEDIENCE STUDY

Stanley Milgram is perhaps most well-known for his famous, yet extremely controversial, experiment on obedience. Milgram was fascinated by the effect that authority had on obedience, and believed that people would nearly always obey orders out of a desire to seem cooperative or out of fear, even if this meant going against their better judgment or desires.

Fitting Milgram's Experiment in History

Milgram began his obedience experiment in 1961. Shortly before, the world had been captivated by the trial of Nazi war criminal Adolf Eichmann, who, among other things, was charged with ordering the deaths of millions of Jews. Eichmann's defense in the case was that he was just following instructions.

Milgram conducted the experiment at Yale University, where he recruited forty men through newspaper ads. The participants were informed (falsely) that the study they were joining was focused on memory and learning. They were told that one person would take on the role of teacher and the other would take on the role of student, and that these roles would be chosen randomly. Each participant drew a supposedly random slip of paper. In reality, however, all of the papers said "teacher" on them. The only "students" were actor accomplices of Milgram's. Thus, all of the unknowing participants were intentionally given the role of the teacher, while believing it to be a random assignment.

EXPERIMENT

MILGRAM'S EXPERIMENT

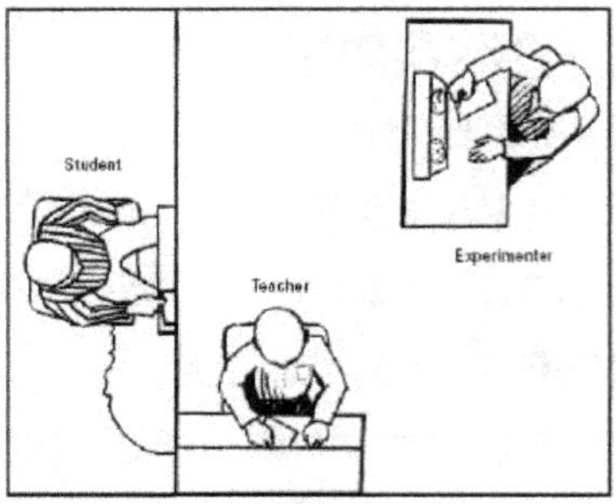

A VISUALIZATION OF MILGRAM'S EXPERIMENT

1. Each participant "teacher" is paired with one of the accomplice "students." The teacher watches as the student is strapped to a chair and has electrodes attached to him by laboratory assistants.
2. Following this, the teacher is then brought into a separate room, where he can still communicate with the student, but they cannot see each other. The teacher is placed in front of a "shock generator" that starts at 30 volts and increases—in increments of 15 volts—all the way to 450 volts. The switches are labeled "Moderate," which is 75–120 volts; "Strong," which is 135–180 volts;

"Danger: Severe Shock," which is 375–420 volts; and the two highest levels are labeled "XXX." The "shock generator" does not produce actual shocks, but rather makes a noise when switches are pressed.

3. The teacher is told that he will teach word pairs to the student and that if the student makes a mistake, the teacher will punish the student by administering a shock. For every mistake made, the teacher must administer a shock 15 volts higher than the last. To show that the experiment is real, the teacher is given a 15 volt shock. This is the only real shock administered in the entire test.
4. The word pairings begin, and the student will eventually begin to make planned errors. At each error, the teacher increases the voltage of the shock that he gives to the student. When the fake shocks reach 75 volts, the "student" will grunt. At 120 volts, the student will complain that the

shocks are painful. At 150 volts, the student will scream that he wants to be released. The student will then plead more and more as the shocks are "administered" and complain that he suffers from a heart condition.

5. If at any time the teacher questions the process, the experimenter will tell him things like "please continue," "it is absolutely essential that you continue," "the experiment requires that you continue," or "you have no other choice, you must go on."
6. At 300 volts, the student pounds on the walls and exclaims that he can't stand the pain. At 330 volts, the student remains quiet. The experimenter informs the teacher that a lack of response is a wrong answer, and that he has to shock the student.
7. The experiment ends when the highest level on the shock generator is reached.

MILGRAM'S FINDINGS

Milgram asked a group of Yale students to predict how many people they thought would administer the maximum shock level, and they estimated three out of 100 people would do it. Surprisingly, Milgram found that 65 percent of the participants in his study administered shock levels of 450 volts! While people did show signs of internal struggle through groaning, nervous laughter, and trembling, most of them obeyed the experimenter's request to continue with the experiment. When interviewed after the experiment, Milgram asked the participants to rate how painful they believed the shocks actually were, and "extremely painful" was the typical answer. Milgram even found that the participants—in an effort to justify their behavior—devalued the student during the experiment, saying the student was so dumb that he actually deserved the shock. Milgram was able to successfully show that under certain circumstances, everyday people who are considered "normal" have the capability to cause intense pain and suffering. Milgram was able to explain such high levels of obedience in the following ways:

- Compliance was increased because of the physical presence of an authority figure (the experimenter)
- Many participants believed the experiment was safe because it was sponsored by Yale
- The selection process of who would be teacher and who would be student seemed random
- It was assumed that the experimenter was a competent expert
- The participants were told the shocks were painful but not dangerous

Ethical Concerns

Milgram's obedience study drew fierce criticism regarding its ethical procedure. The subjects involved in the study were led to believe that they were causing pain to another person when, in reality, they were being duped by an actor pretending to be in pain. The experiment caused great stress to the subjects, and the fact that they believed they were hurting a complete stranger could have traumatized them.

SMALL WORLD EXPERIMENT

Despite being most famous for his obedience study, Milgram also participated in several more benign experiments. Have you ever heard of the term "six degrees of separation"? If so, you can thank Stanley Milgram for that.

In the 1950s, political scientist Ithiel de Sola Pool and mathematician Manfred Kochen posed several questions: What would be the probability of two complete strangers having a mutual friend? What if there were no mutual friend? How long would that chain be for them to reach each other? Approximately a decade later, Stanley Milgram conducted an experiment known as "The Small World Experiment" in an effort to answer these questions.

Milgram gave 300 letters with instructions to people in Omaha, Nebraska, and Wichita, Kansas, and set up one "target" in Boston, Massachusetts. The 300 people were told to mail the letter to a friend that they thought was close to the target (and that they knew on a first name basis), and this friend would get the same instructions, creating a chain. Milgram received a postcard with each forward and recorded the relationship between sender and receiver. Milgram discovered that within almost all instances, the chains had approximately five or six links that connected any two people.

Stanley Milgram brought great—and sometimes scary—insight to humanity in ways that many had never seen before. While his controversial (and now classic) obedience study showed the rather negative side of what an individual could be capable of doing, his small world experiment was able to show the interconnectivity and closeness that people share. To this day, his work continues to be incredibly influential and extremely important, and he is firmly planted as one of the most discussed psychologists in the history of psychology and experimentation.

ALFRED ADLER (1870–1937)

It's all about the individual

Alfred Adler was born on February 7th, 1870, in Vienna, Austria, to the family of a Jewish grain merchant. Adler had suffered from rickets as a child, and because of this did not learn how to walk until the age of four. When Adler was five years old, he developed pneumonia and almost died from the condition. His early experiences with illness sparked an interest in medicine and inspired him to pursue a career as a physician.

Following school, he worked as an ophthalmologist and eventually switched to general practice. Adler set up his office in the lower class part of Vienna, and across the street from his office was an amusement park and circus. As a result, most of the clients he saw were circus performers. By studying the unusual strengths and weaknesses that these circus performers had, Adler began to create his organ inferiority theory, wherein he posited that a person with a particular defect of a physical nature will experience feelings of shortcoming or inferiority because of this handicap, and will attempt to compensate for the weakness. This would later prove to have a large impact on some of his most important work in psychology.

Over time, Adler began to shift away from ophthalmology and towards psychology. By 1907, he was invited to join discussion groups led by Sigmund Freud. These meetings would eventually turn into the Vienna Psychoanalytic Society, and Sigmund Freud would name Adler president and co-editor of the organization's newsletter.

Though he was president, Adler was very vocal about his disagreements with several of Freud's theories. Eventually, a debate between supporters of Freud and supporters of Adler was held, and Adler, along with nine other members, resigned from the Vienna Psychoanalytic Society. They would go on to form the Society for Free Psychoanalysis in 1911, which a year later would become The Society for Individual Psychology.

While Adler played a major role in the development of psychoanalysis with Freud, he was one of the first to break away from the school of thought and create his own, which he called Individual Psychology. One of the most influential ideas to come out of this school of thought was the notion of the inferiority complex, which suggested that personality and behavior were the result of people working to overcome an inherent sense of inferiority.

When World War I broke out, Adler worked as a physician on the Russian front, and then for a children's hospital. During World War II, even though Adler had converted to Christianity, the Nazis closed down his clinics as a result of his Jewish heritage, and Adler came to the United States and accepted a professor position at the Long Island College of Medicine. On May 28th, 1937, while on a lecture tour, Alfred Adler had a severe heart attack and died. His contributions to the field, however, endured long after his sudden death, and shaped much of the discussion of the next half-century of psychological thought.

INDIVIDUAL PSYCHOLOGY

Where Freud believed that there were universal biological factors that made people behave in certain ways, Alfred Adler believed that behaviors were based on the individual's experiences and environmental and societal factors. Personality was determined by the confrontation of love-related, vocational, and societal forces.

Essentially, Adler believed that every person was unique and none of the previous theories could be applied to every single person. It is for this reason that Adler called his theory "Individual Psychology." Adler's theory is extremely complex because it covers a wide range of psychological topics; however, the central principle of individual psychology is extremely simple because it follows one notion: striving for success or superiority.

STRIVING FOR SUCCESS AND SUPERIORITY

Adler firmly believed that the driving forces behind a person's actions were the desire for personal gain, which he called superiority, and the desire for community benefit, which he called success. Due to the fact that all people are born with small, delicate, and inferior bodies, we develop a sense of inferiority and attempt to overcome these feelings. People who strive for superiority have little concern for others and are only focused on personal benefit, and are therefore psychologically unhealthy. People who strive for success do so for all of humanity without losing their identity, and are therefore psychologically healthy.

Doctoral Definitions

Inferiority Complex: A wholly or partly unconscious sense of inferiority, or feelings of lack of worth. The overcompensation of these feelings can lead to neurotic symptoms.

Superiority Complex:
Suppressing feelings that exist in an attempt to conquer an inferiority complex.

According to Adler, an individual's personality traits are derived from these external factors:

1. **Compensation:** When a person suffers from a disadvantage, they are made inferior to others and aim to put an end to those disadvantages. People who are able to do so become successful on an individual and social basis.
2. **Resignation:** This happens when people give in to their disadvantages and settle with them. This occurs with the majority of people.
3. **Overcompensation:** This occurs when a person becomes infatuated with the notion of compensating for their weaknesses or disadvantages and

they overindulge in the pursuit of striving for success. These people, Adler stated, were neurotics.

Alfred Adler introduced the world to ideas that were drastically different than those of Sigmund Freud by focusing on the uniqueness of the individual, instead of simply concentrating on a set of universal biological factors like Freud. By differentiating himself from Freud and his contemporaries, he offered a competing vision of psychological development, especially in children, and established principles that are still considered bedrocks to the modern interpretations of psychology.

BASIC THEORIES ON GROUPS

What happens when people come together

Though a person might not realize it, groups have a very powerful and dramatic effect on human behavior. Everyone acts differently when they are around people versus than when they are alone.

SOCIAL FACILITATION

The most basic theory regarding social psychology is that when a person is alone, he or she is more relaxed and not concerned about the appearance of their behavior. By adding just one other person to the equation, behaviors begin to change and people become more aware of what is going on around them. As a result, studies have shown that a person will be able to perform tasks that are simple or well-learned with a greater performance level. However, when attempting to do something that is new or difficult around another person, performance level will decrease. This is known as social facilitation: due to the presence of other people, we try harder and our performance level actually declines in new or difficult tasks.

Take basketball as an example. If you are just beginning to learn basketball, you will feel more relaxed practicing alone than practicing around other people, because the presence of others will make you feel self-conscious and you will make more mistakes. If you are a professional basketball player, however, you are already skilled in the task, and the presence of other people will make you better as you strive to demonstrate your ability.

WHEN GROUPS MAKE DECISIONS

When groups make decisions, one of two things generally happens: “groupthink” or “group polarization.”

Groupthink

When a group agrees on most issues, there is a tendency to stifle any dissent. The group anticipates harmony. If everyone agrees and is content, they do not appreciate hearing opposing arguments. Groupthink can be disastrous because it leads to a failure to listen to or identify all sides of an argument and can result in impulsive decisions. Examples of groupthink gone wrong include mass riots and lynch mobs. To combat groupthink, authentic dissent should be nurtured.

Group Polarization

This takes root when a group begins to create extreme positions that are fueled by the group and would not have occurred if any of the individuals were alone. For example, at the beginning of a decision-making process, perhaps members of the group were only slightly opposed to something. By the end of the discussion together, however, the entire group is now dramatically opposed to the issue and has taken this opposition to an extreme level. To reduce group polarization, homogeneity should be avoided.

BYSTANDER EFFECT

The bystander effect is perhaps the most tragic phenomenon to occur within groups. It has been found that as a group gets larger, the internal drive to help other people in need actually decreases. Though this is similar to social loafing, the bystander effect occurs because people become followers and will only help someone if they see another individual helping in the first place. Note: this is strictly a group phenomenon. If there is no one else present but one individual and the victim, that individual will usually help the victim.

One of the Most Famous Examples of the Bystander Effect

On March 13th, 1964, at 3:20 A.M., twenty-eight-year-old Catherine "Kitty" Genovese was coming home from work and was approached by a man in her apartment entrance. The man attacked and stabbed Genovese. Genovese repeatedly called for help, but not a single one of the close to forty eyewitnesses who had heard her cries for help and watched the events unfold called the police. Instead, they all believed that someone else was doing it. It wasn't until 3:50 A.M. that the police were finally contacted.

RULES OF GROUPS

No matter what type of group it is, whether it be a band, a group of friends, a work meeting, a sports team, or something else, all groups share similar psychological processes and follow certain rules.

1. **Groups can come from nearly nothing:** Groups contribute to our sense of ourselves; because of this, it is in our nature to want to form and build groups.

2. **There usually is some form of initiation rite:** If someone is joining an already existing group, there is usually some form of initiation rite. This could be intellectual, monetary, physical, or based on similar experiences. Groups want to test individuals entering, and they want the membership to the group to be valued.
3. **Groups create conformity:** Groups have certain norms that members follow and these norms can bend an individual's behavior, making them go against their better judgment (for one of the greatest examples, see Asch's Conformity Study).
4. **You must learn the norms of the group:** If you break the rules established by the group, the other members of the group will be sure to let you know.
5. **People take on roles within groups:** While there are rules that apply to everyone within a group,

individuals will also begin taking on specific roles and follow a set of rules associated with those roles.

6. **Most of the time, leaders emerge from the group slowly:** Though leaders can be appointed and imposed upon, most of the time leaders emerge by first conforming to the group; and then after gaining trust, they become more confident and eventually others will follow them.
7. **Groups create improved performance:** The presence of other people can make an individual perform better. This is more likely when the task at hand is separate from other people's tasks and the individual can be judged on his or her own merits.
8. **There will be rumors and, most of the time, they will be true:** In 1985, a study took place in a work environment and found that people talked of rumors and gossip 80 percent of the time, and that an astounding 80 percent

of this information was true. Other studies have shown very similar results.

9. **Groups create competition:** People in groups can become suspicious and wary of the people in rivaling groups. This creates an "us vs. them" type of situation, and even if an individual from a rival group is thought of as cooperative, the group as a whole is deemed untrustworthy or bad.

Groups play an incredibly important role in everyday life and dramatically impact the decisions we make. A group can be anything from a meeting of coworkers responsible for making important financial decisions to a group of friends deciding on where they would like to eat their next meal. The mere presence of other people has a remarkable effect on our behavior. A group can occur from nothing, make some perform better, make others choose not to perform, and create roles and norms that group members follow.

PHILIP ZIMBARDO

(1933–PRESENT)

The man who created a prison

Philip Zimbardo was born on March 23rd, 1933, in New York City. In 1954, Zimbardo earned his bachelor's degree from Brooklyn College, where he triple-majored in psychology, sociology, and anthropology. He then attended Yale, where he earned his MA in psychology in 1955, and his PhD in psychology in 1959.

After briefly teaching at Yale, Zimbardo taught as a psychology professor at New York University until 1967. He then spent a year teaching at Columbia University; and in 1968, he became a faculty member at Stanford University, where he remained until his retirement in 2003 (though his last lecture was given in 2007). It was at Stanford University that Zimbardo's most important and influential work, the Stanford Prison Experiment, was performed in 1971.

While the Stanford Prison Experiment is what he is most known for, Zimbardo has also conducted research on heroism, shyness, and cult behavior, and has published over fifty books. Zimbardo was elected president of the American Psychological Association in 2002 and is the founder of the Heroic Imagination Project. The Project aims to inspire heroic behavior and to understand what makes some people turn towards acts of evil while others turn towards acts of heroism.

THE STANFORD PRISON EXPERIMENT

In 1971, Philip Zimbardo created an experiment to understand abusive behavior within the prison system and to learn how situations can impact human behavior. He posed the question: what would happen if dignity and individuality were stripped away from individuals? The result was the infamous Stanford Prison Experiment: one of the most telling experiments produced in the field of psychology.

Zimbardo and his team transformed the basement of the Stanford University psychology department into a mock prison. He advertised in the local papers for participants, offering $15 a day for a two-week study. Of the respondents, twenty-four male subjects were chosen that were deemed to be emotionally and mentally sound, and were mostly middle class and white. The twenty-four men were then randomly divided into two groups: twelve prison guards and twelve prisoners. Zimbardo was to act as warden of the prison.

Dressed for the Occasion

The prison guards were dressed in military-style uniforms and sunglasses (to prevent eye contact), and were each given wooden batons to establish their status. The prisoners were to wear stocking caps, uncomfortable smocks, no underwear, and were only allowed to go by identification numbers, not names. They also wore a small chain on one leg as a reminder that they were inmates. Inside of their prison cells, they were only given a mattress and plain food.

Before the experiment began, the prisoners were told to go back to their homes and await further instruction. When home, without any warning, their homes were raided by actual local police (who had agreed to help in the experiment), and they were each charged with armed robbery. They were then read their rights, had fingerprints and mug shots taken, and were stripped, searched, deloused, and brought into their prison cells, where they would spend the next two weeks. There were three prisoners to each cell, and prisoners were required to stay in the cell day and night. The prison guards, however, did not have to stay once their shift ended, and they were given free reign to run the prison however they wanted, with the only exception being no physical punishment.

THE RESULTS

The Stanford Prison Experiment was forced to stop just six days into the two-week study. By the second day, prisoners in Cell 1 used their mattresses to blockade the door. Guards from different shifts volunteered to work to suppress the riot and used fire extinguishers on the prisoners.

The guards then decided to create a "privilege cell," where prisoners not involved in the riot would be given a special reward, such as a meal that was of better quality. The prisoners in the "privilege cell," however, refused to eat the food and stayed in solidarity with their fellow inmates.

A mere thirty-six hours into the study, one prisoner, #8612, began screaming wildly, cursing, and got so out of control that Zimbardo saw no other choice but to release him.

The prison guards began punishing the prisoners by making them repeat their assigned numbers, forcing them to exercise, and confiscating their mattresses so they had no choice but to sleep on the hard, cold concrete. The prison guards turned the use of the toilet into a privilege and frequently denied bathroom access to the prisoners, instead giving them a bucket in their cells. They also made the prisoners clean the toilet with their bare hands. In an effort to humiliate the prisoners, some were forced to strip completely naked.

One-third of the prison guards showed sadistic tendencies, and even Zimbardo himself became immersed in his role as prison ward. On day four, there were rumors that the prisoner who had been released was going to come back to free the remaining prisoners. Zimbardo and the guards moved the prison to another floor, and Zimbardo waited in the basement in case the prisoner returned, where he would tell him that the experiment ended early. The prisoner never showed, however, and the prison was once again rebuilt in the basement.

When a new prisoner was introduced, he was given the instructions to go on a hunger strike in response to the treatment of his fellow prisoners. Instead of viewing him as a fellow victim, the other prisoners saw this new prisoner as a troublemaker. The prison guards put the new prisoner in solitary confinement and gave the rest of the prisoners an option: they could give up their blankets to let the man out of solitary confinement. Everyone except for one prisoner decided to keep their blankets.

Surprisingly, none of the inmates wanted to quit early, even when they were told they would not get the money for participating. Zimbardo concluded that the prisoners had internalized and adopted their roles, becoming institutionalized.

After six days of the experiment, a graduate student was brought in to interview the prisoners and guards, and was absolutely shocked by what she saw. As a result of this outside perspective, Zimbardo ended the experiment. He noted that of the fifty visitors, she was the only person to have questioned the morality of the experiment.

The Stanford Prison Experiment is one of the most important and controversial psychological experiments to ever have been conducted. Under the current Ethics Code of the American Psychological Association, the experiment could not be replicated because it does not meet many of today's ethical standards. However, Zimbardo successfully showed how behavior could be influenced by the situation a person is in, and there are numerous real-world examples that prove Zimbardo's work, including the abuse of prisoners at Abu Ghraib in Iraq.

SOLOMON ASCH (1907–1996)

The power of social influence

Solomon Asch was born on September 14th, 1907, in Warsaw, Poland, to a Jewish family. When Asch was thirteen years old, his family uprooted to the United States to reside in the Lower East Side of Manhattan. Asch earned his bachelor's degree from the College of the City of New York in 1928. From there, Asch attended Columbia University, where he would study under Max Wertheimer and earn his MA in 1930, and his PhD in 1932. Asch then became a professor of psychology at Swarthmore College, where he stayed for nineteen years and worked with fellow Gestalt psychologist Wolfgang Köhler.

In the 1950s, Asch gained widespread attention for his research on social psychology and his groundbreaking series of experiments known as the Asch Conformity Experiments. These experiments helped thrust him into the academic spotlight and established several longstanding theories about social influence.

From 1966 to 1972, Asch was director of the Institute for Cognitive Studies at Rutgers University. He was an emeritus professor of psychology at the University of Pennsylvania starting in 1979, and professor of psychology there from 1972 to 1979.

Solomon Asch died on February 20th, 1996. He was eighty-eight years old.

EXPERIMENT

ASCH'S CONFORMITY EXPERIMENTS

In 1951, Solomon Asch created an experiment to understand how social pressures from a majority would make a single individual conform. Asch's Conformity Experiments are some of the most famous experiments in psychology, and are incredibly easy to replicate.

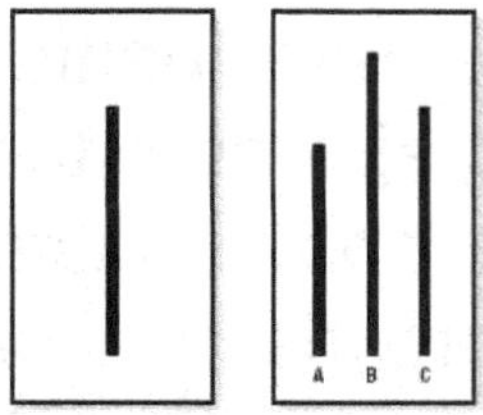

SAMPLE CARD FROM THE ASCH CONFORMITY EXPERIMENTS

1. Have six to eight people participate in the study. All but one of the people will be confederates, or accomplices, but they will not make this fact known to the one test subject that is not a confederate. The accomplices should seem like real participants to the test subject.
2. There will be a series of eighteen simple visual questions, where the answer should always be obvious. All of your participants will answer each question in the presence of each other.
3. Sit the participants in a line, and have the test subject sit at the end and be the last or second to last to give his or her answer.

4. Show the participants a card with a line on it, similar to the card on the left in the above illustration. Then show them the card on the right, with the three lines labeled A, B, and C.
5. Have each person say out loud which one out of A, B, or C is most similar to the line on the left.
6. The first two answers should be correct, so the test subject feels comfortable.
7. On the third answer, the confederates should all start giving the same wrong answer.
8. Out of the eighteen trials, the confederates should answer twelve of them with the same incorrect answer. These twelve are the "critical trials."
9. The goal of this experiment is to see if the test subject will begin giving the same answer as the rest of the group even though it is the wrong answer.

THE RESULTS

Amazingly, Asch found that over the eighteen trials, 75 percent of participants conformed at least once to the clearly incorrect answer given by the majority of the group. After combing the trials, Asch concluded that 32 percent of the participants conformed. To make sure that the individuals accurately understood the length of the lines, Asch had them write down what they thought was the correct match, and 98 percent of the time, the participants chose the correct match. This percentage was higher because the pressure from being in the group was no longer an issue.

Asch also looked at how the number of people that were present affected conformity. When there was only one other person with the test subject, there was practically no impact on the answers given by the test subject. And when there were two other people present, there was a small effect. When there were three or more confederates, however, the results were much more significant.

When the comparison lines were harder to judge because their lengths were very similar, Asch discovered that conformity increased. This demonstrates that when people are unsure about something, they are more likely to turn to other people for a confirmation. The more difficult the task is, the greater the chance of having conformity.

Asch also discovered that if only one confederate gave the correct answer while the rest of the confederates still gave the wrong answer, conformity was dramatically lower (only 5–10 percent of the test subjects conformed). This shows that social support can play a key role in fighting conformity.

THOUGHTS ON CONFORMITY

When the experiment was over, the test subjects were asked why they had followed along with what the rest of the group was saying. Most of the time, the test subjects replied by saying that they knew the answer was incorrect but they did not want to risk being ridiculed. Others responded that they actually believed what the group was saying was true.

What does the Asch experiment tell us about conformity? Conformity occurs for two main reasons: either because people want to fit in—this is known as normative influence—or because of informational influence, where people believe the group *must* be more informed or understand more than they do. Both types of influence can have powerful impacts on individuals within a group setting. While many psychologists may have suspected that group dynamics could influence individual perception, it was not until Asch conducted his famous experiment that the world finally understood just how much perception could be altered by outside pressure.

JOHN B. WATSON

(1878–1958)

Founder of behaviorism

John Broadus Watson was born on January 9th, 1878, in South Carolina. Watson's father left the family when he was just thirteen years old, forcing Watson to grow up on a farm in poverty and isolation. Watson claimed he was a poor and unruly student as a child, and that he seemed destined to follow in his father's footsteps of a life ruled by recklessness and violence. At the age of sixteen, however, Watson enrolled at Furman University.

Watson would graduate five years later and move on to the University of Chicago to earn a doctorate degree in psychology and philosophy. By 1903, Watson had dropped philosophy and received his PhD in psychology. In 1908, he began teaching at Johns Hopkins University as a professor of experimental and comparative psychology.

By this time, Watson was already beginning to form ideas on what would later become a completely new branch of psychology: behaviorism. Inspired by the work of Ivan Pavlov, Watson began studying physiology, biology, animal behavior, and the behavior of children. Watson believed that children operated on the same principles that animals did, though they were simply more complicated beings. Watson concluded that every animal was a very complex machine that responded to situations based on its "wiring," the nerve pathways that had been conditioned through experience.

In 1913, Watson gave a lecture at Columbia University called "Psychology as the Behaviorist Views It." This lecture called for an extreme revision of the methods of research in psychology, abandoning introspection for the study of behavior and calling for behavior to be evaluated separate from consciousness. He called for psychology to not make distinctions between animal and human behavior and for it to be an objective, natural science where one could develop principles by which behavior could not only be predicted, but also controlled. In addition, Watson dismissed the idea that a significant factor in behavior was heredity and disagreed with the structural ideas of Sigmund Freud. This lecture was later published as an article in the *Psychological Review* that same year and would become known as the "behaviorist manifesto."

Watson worked at Johns Hopkins University until 1920, when he was asked to resign because of an affair he was having with his research associate. By 1924, with his wealth of knowledge in human behavior and psychology, Watson went into advertising and became vice president at one of the largest advertising agencies in the United States, J. Walter Thompson.

Watson spent the last five years of his life living as a recluse on a farm in Connecticut, and his already troubled relationship with his children grew worse. Shortly before dying, Watson burned many of his letters and unpublished papers. He died on September 25th, 1958.

Behaviorism

In behaviorism, it is believed that a person is passive and simply responds to environmental stimuli through conditioning (both classical and operant). In essence, an individual is a clean slate and their behavior is the result of either positive or negative reinforcement. Because behavior can be observed, it is much easier to collect and quantify data. Though behaviorism is no longer as popular as it had been in the mid-twentieth century, its influence can still be found in parenting methods, teaching methods, animal training, and changing practices in people that are harmful or maladaptive.

THE LITTLE ALBERT EXPERIMENT

John B. Watson took a great interest in Ivan Pavlov's experiment on dogs and conditioning, and wanted to see if he could take behavioral conditioning one step further by classically conditioning emotional reactions in people.

The participant of the experiment was a nearly nine-month-old baby that Watson referred to as "Albert B.," but who is now commonly referred to as Little Albert. Watson and his research assistant, Rosalie Raynor—whom Watson would have an affair with—exposed the baby to a variety of stimuli and recorded the baby's reactions. The stimuli included a rabbit, a monkey, a white rat, burning newspapers, and masks. At first, the child showed absolutely no fear to any of the stimuli.

The next time Watson exposed the child to the white rat, he simultaneously used a hammer and hit a metal pipe, which created an extremely loud noise. The baby began to cry from the noise. Watson then repeated the pairing of the loud noise with the white rat. Eventually, the baby began crying just from seeing the white rat, without any noise being paired with it.

- The neutral stimulus was the white rat
- The unconditioned stimulus was the loud noise created by the hammer hitting the metal pipe
- The unconditioned response was fear
- The conditioned stimulus was the white rat
- The conditioned response was fear

As with Pavlov, Watson had shown that it was possible to create a conditioned response to a neutral stimulus; although in Watson's case, the conditioned response was taking place in a human and it was an emotional, not merely physiological, response. Furthermore, Watson also noticed a new fearful reaction in Little Albert to all white objects, which came to be known as stimulus generalization.

For example, following conditioning, the baby in the Little Albert experiment not only became afraid when it saw the white rat but also a variety of white objects, from a white fur coat to a Santa Claus beard.

Doctoral Definitions

Stimulus Generalization: When a subject responds to stimuli that are similar to the original conditioned stimulus but are not identical.

CRITICISMS OF THE EXPERIMENT

Though it was a landmark experiment in psychology, Watson's Little Albert experiment has been criticized for several reasons. The baby's reactions were not evaluated objectively but were simply the subjective interpretations of Watson and Raynor, and the experiment raises many ethical questions. Today, if someone were to try this experiment, it would be considered unethical by the American Psychological Association because it evokes fear in a person, and that is only ethical if the person agrees to participate in the study knowing in advance that they will be purposely scared as part of the experiment. Regardless, behavioral psychologists were able to derive many important insights from Watson and from the results of the Little Albert experiment that have continued to shape the field.

HERMANN RORSCHACH (1884–1922)

Personality through inkblots

Hermann Rorschach was born on November 8th, 1884, in Zurich, Switzerland, and was the oldest son of a failed artist who made a living as an art teacher. Even as a young child, Rorschach was fascinated with inkblots (probably the result of his father's artistic endeavors and his own passion for art), and in secondary school, he went by the nickname "Klex," which literally meant "inkblot." When Rorschach was twelve years old, his mother died, and when he was eighteen years old, his father died.

Following high school, which he graduated from with honors, Rorschach went to college to earn a medical degree. In 1912, Rorschach earned his MD from the University of Zurich and began working in various mental institutions.

In 1911, while training at the University of Zurich, Rorschach performed experiments on schoolchildren using inkblots to see if those children that were more gifted artistically were also more imaginative when it came to their interpretations of the inkblots. This would prove to not only have a dramatic impact on Rorschach's studies, but also on the entire field of psychology. While Rorschach was not the first to incorporate inkblots into his work, this experiment was the first time inkblots were significantly used in an analytical approach. The results of this experiment have since been lost, but for the next ten years, Rorschach conducted research in an effort to create a consistent method that would lead to the understanding of personality traits by simply using inkblots.

Because he was employed at a mental hospital, Rorschach had easy access to patients. Along with using mentally and emotionally stable and healthy individuals, Rorschach was able to create a systematic test using inkblots that could analyze a person and give significant results on their personality traits.

In 1921, Rorschach presented his work with the publishing of his book,

Psychodiagnostik. In his book, Rorschach also goes over his own theories of personality. One of his main arguments is that all people have a mixture of introversive and extratensive personalities—they are motivated by both internal and external influences. Rorschach believed that through the inkblot test, the relative amount of these personality traits could be measured, which could help reveal any mental abnormalities or strengths.

When Rorschach's book first came out, it was largely ignored by the psychiatric community because the common belief at that time was that personality could not be measured or tested. By 1922, psychiatrists began seeing the benefits of Rorschach's test, and Rorschach discussed improving the test at a meeting of the Psychoanalytic Society. On April 1st, 1922, after a week of suffering from abdominal pains, Rorschach was admitted into the hospital for appendicitis. On April 2nd, 1922, Hermann Rorschach died. He was only thirty-seven years old and never got to see the success of his inkblot test.

THE RORSCHACH INKBLOTS

The Rorschach test consists of ten inkblots in total: five are black ink, two are red and black ink, and three are multicolored. A psychologist will present each card in a very specific order and then ask the patient, “What might this be?” Once the patient has viewed all of the inkblots and has given his or her thoughts, the psychologist will then show the inkblots to the patient again, one at a time. The patient is told to list everything he or she sees, where they see it, and what in the inkblot makes them say that. The inkblot can be rotated, tilted, turned upside down, or manipulated in any manner of ways. The psychologist should record everything that the patient says and does, as well as time each of the responses. Responses are then analyzed and scored. Through a series of mathematical calculations, a summary of the test data is produced and interpreted using empirical data.

If you have no initial reaction or you can’t seem to describe the card you are looking at, this may mean that you have a block in the subject that the card is representative of, or the card deals with a topic that you don't want to confront at that point in time.

Card 1

The first card is just made up of black ink. Because this is the first card a person will see, this can provide insight into how the patient will take on a task that is new and stressful. People will often describe this card as looking like a bat, moth, butterfly, or the face of some kind of animal, like an elephant or rabbit. This card generally reflects the person.

- While a bat can mean something unclean or demonic for some, for others it can mean navigating through darkness and rebirth.
- Butterflies can symbolize transition, transformation, as well as the ability to grow, change, and overcome.
- Moths can symbolize feeling overlooked, ugly, as well as our weaknesses and annoyances.
- The face of an animal, in particular an elephant, can symbolize the

ways in which we confront problems, and a fear of looking into our inner issues. It can also symbolize "the elephant in the room," and comment on an issue that is being tiptoed around.

Card 2

This card consists of red and black ink, and is often perceived as sexual in nature. The parts that are red are usually interpreted as blood, and the way a person responds can reflect the ways in which he or she manages feelings, physical harm, or anger. People will often describe this card as resembling praying, two people, a person looking in the mirror, or four-legged animals like a dog, bear, or elephant.

- Seeing two people can symbolize codependency, an obsession with sex, ambivalent feelings about sex, or a focus on bonding with other people or relationships.
- Seeing a person looking at their reflection in the mirror can symbolize self-absorption or self-

reflection. Either can be a negative or positive trait, depending on the person's feelings.

- Seeing a dog can symbolize an affectionate and loyal friend. If the patient has just seen something negative, this could indicate that they need to face their fears and acknowledge inner feelings.
- Seeing an elephant can symbolize thoughtfulness, memory, and intelligence; however, it can also symbolize a negative physical self-image.
- Seeing a bear can symbolize aggression, competition, independence, resurrection, and can even be a play on the word "bare," which may mean feelings of vulnerability, being unprotected, or feeling sincere and honest.
- This card is extremely sexual, so seeing a person praying may symbolize a person's beliefs about sex within the context of their religion. The blood can also indicate that a person associates physical pain with religion, that the person

turns to prayer when undergoing challenging emotions such as anger, or that the person associates anger with religion.

Card 3

The third card features red and black ink, and symbolizes how a person relates to other people in social interactions. Common responses to this card include seeing two people, one person looking into a mirror, a butterfly, or a moth.

- Seeing two people eating with one another symbolizes that the participant's social life is nourishing. Seeing two people washing their hands can symbolize insecurity, a sense of not being clean, or paranoid feelings. Viewing two people participating in some form of game can indicate a competitive view of social relationships.
- Seeing a person looking at their reflection in the mirror can symbolize self-absorption, being oblivious to others, or not seeing people for who they are.

Card 4

The fourth card is often known as the "father card." It is composed of black ink and features shading. Often viewed as a large and sometimes intimidating or frightening figure that is categorized as male more than female, this inkblot relates to the person's feelings towards authority and their upbringing. Common responses include seeing a large animal or monster, or seeing animal hide or animal skin.

- Seeing a large animal or monster can symbolize feelings of inferiority towards authority, or amplified fear of authority figures, including father figures.
- Seeing animal hide or animal skin can symbolize great discomfort when discussing the subject of the father. On the opposite end, it can symbolize that the individual has less of a problem with authority and inferiority.

Card 5

This card is made up of black ink and once again, just like the very first card, reflects us. This card is usually not considered to be threatening, and since the previous cards offered more of a challenge, this card should be relatively easy for the person and will produce a quality response. If the answers are not similar to the answers given for the first card, this means that cards 2–4 have possibly influenced the individual. Common responses to this card include a bat, butterfly, or moth.

Card 6

This card is made up of black ink, and the dominant characteristic of the card is the texture of the inkblot. This card elicits an association with interpersonal closeness, and for this reason, it is known as the "sex card." The most common response to this card is an animal hide or skin, which can indicate a resistance to being close and, as a result, a feeling of personal emptiness and disconnectedness.

Card 7

This card is made up of black ink and is usually linked to femininity. Due to the fact that common responses to this card include women and children, this is known as the "mother card." If the person has problems responding to this card, it can be due to problems they are facing with female figures in their life. Common responses to this card include heads or faces of women or children, and kissing.

- Seeing the heads of women symbolizes feelings associated with one's view of his or her mother. These feelings will also influence their views of women overall.
- Seeing the heads of children symbolizes feelings associated with childhood and the need to care for the inner child. This can also indicate that the relationship that the participant has with their mother needs to be looked at and healed.
- Seeing heads about to kiss symbolizes the desire for affection and reconnection with a mother figure. This can indicate that there

was once a close relationship with the mother that it is now sought in other relationships, be they romantic or social.

Card 8

This card is extremely colorful and features gray, pink, orange, and blue ink. Not only is this the first card that is multicolored, but it is also extremely complex. If this card or the change of pace makes the participant uncomfortable, they might have trouble processing complex situations or emotional stimuli. Common responses to this card include seeing four-legged animals, a butterfly, or a moth.

Card 9

This card is made up of green, pink, and orange inks. This inkblot is characterized by its vagueness and the inability to visualize a specific thing. Most people struggle to find what they see in it. It is for this reason that this card explores how well a person handles a lack of structure and vagueness. Common responses to come out of this card are either a generic human form or some indeterminate evil shape.

- If a human is viewed, the way the individual feels about this person can symbolize how the participant deals with unstructured time and information.
- Seeing evil could symbolize that in order to feel comfort, structure is required in the participant's life, and that they don't tolerate vagueness well.

Card 10

The last card in the Rorschach test is the most colorful, with orange, yellow, pink, green, gray, and blue inks. Structurally speaking, this card is similar to card 8, but it has a complexity similar to card 9. And while many find this card to be pleasant, those who do not enjoy the complexity of card 9 may feel the same way with this card, which can indicate a difficulty in dealing with similar, synchronous, or coincidental stimuli. Common responses to this inkblot include crab, lobster, spider, a rabbit head, snakes, or caterpillars.

- Seeing a crab can either symbolize a tendency to cling onto things or other people, or it can symbolize perseverance.
- Seeing a lobster can symbolize strength, perseverance, and an ability to conquer small problems. A lobster can also symbolize a fear of harming oneself or of being harmed.
- Seeing a spider can symbolize fear, a feeling of entanglement, or a feeling of being trapped in an uncomfortable situation as a result of telling lies. It can also symbolize an overbearing mother and feminine power.
- Seeing the head of a rabbit can symbolize fertility and a positive outlook.
- Snakes can symbolize danger, feeling lied to or deceived, or being afraid of the unknown. Snakes can also be considered a phallic symbol

and can relate to unacceptable or forbidden sex.

- Because this card is at the end of the test, seeing caterpillars symbolizes room for growth and an understanding that you are constantly re-inventing yourself and evolving.

VISUAL PERCEPTION

How you're seeing what you're seeing

Humans receive information with sense organs, including their ears, nose, and eyes. These organs are part of larger sensory systems that receive information and send information to the brain. In visual perception, psychologists attempt to figure out how the information transmitted from the sense organs creates the foundation of perception. In other words, psychologists attempt to explain why, for example, you perceive a chair when the light hits your eye or why, when a sound wave comes to you, you perceive that sound in a certain way. Psychologists still disagree on the extent to which perception relies upon the information found in the stimulus. The two main theories to explain how we process information are top-down processing and bottom-up processing, both of which have ardent backers in the psychological community.

TOP-DOWN PROCESSING

In 1970, psychologist Richard Gregory claimed that perception was constructive, and that when a person looks at something, they begin to perceptually hypothesize about it based on prior knowledge—and these hypotheses are, for the most part, always correct. Top-down processing is based on pattern recognition and using contextual information. For example, if you are trying to read someone's poor handwriting, it will be harder to understand a single word than it will be to understand a complete sentence, because the meaning of the other words will help you understand by providing context.

Gregory estimated that around 90 percent of information that reaches the eye is lost by the time it gets to the brain. The brain then uses past experiences to construct a perception of reality. Perception involves a large degree of hypothesis testing, so that the information presented by the sense organs can be logical. As sensory receptors get information from the environment, this information is then combined with information on the world that has been previously stored from past experiences.

THE NECKER CUBE

The Necker cube is used to justify and support the hypothesis of top-down processing by showing that incorrect hypotheses will result in errors of perception, like visual illusions.

If you stare at the crosses on the cube, you will notice that its orientation can seemingly flip. This single physical pattern is unstable and actually creates two perceptions.

Top-down adherents claim that the reason for the two perceptions is that the brain has developed two hypotheses that are both equally plausible based on the sensory input and on previous experiences, and it cannot decide between the two.

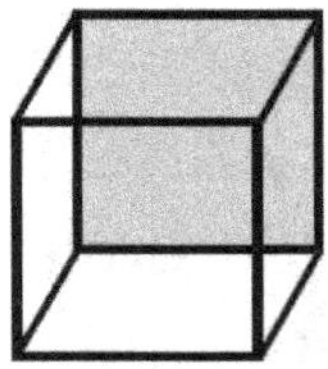

THE NECKER CUBE

BOTTOM-UP PROCESSING

Not all psychologists believe that top-down processing is the correct interpretation of visual stimuli. Psychologist James Gibson disagrees with the claims of hypothesis testing, and claims instead that perception is more direct. Gibson states that sense can be made from the world in a very direct way, because there is enough information in our environment. In Gibson's bottom-up processing, there is not any interpretation or processing of the information received, because this information is detailed enough. To support this argument, one can think about the following scenario: you are sitting on a fast moving train, and as you travel, objects closer to you pass by at a faster rate than objects that are farther away. The distance of faraway objects can be understood by their relative speed. In bottom-up processing (or data-drive processing), perception starts with the stimulus itself and is analyzed in a single direction—a simple breakdown of raw sensory information to increasingly more complex analyses.

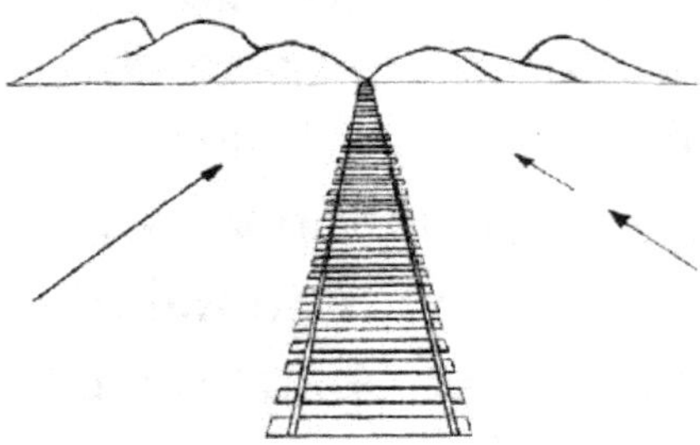

VISUALIZATION FROM THE REAR OF A TRAIN

After working with pilots on the subject of depth perception during World War II, Gibson came to the conclusion that perception of surfaces had more importance than perception of either depth or space, because surfaces have features that allow objects to be distinguished from one another. Gibson also claimed that part of perception was understanding the function of an object—for example, whether the object can be sat on, thrown, or carried.

While working in aviation, Gibson discovered something that he referred to as "optic flow patterns."

As a pilot approaches a landing strip, the point that the pilot is moving towards appears still while the surrounding visual environment seems to actually move away from the point. Gibson claimed that optic flow patterns could give pilots unmistakable information when it came to their speed, direction, and altitude. By using the concept of optic flow patterns, Gibson was able to make a more complete, three-part description of his theory of bottom-up processing.

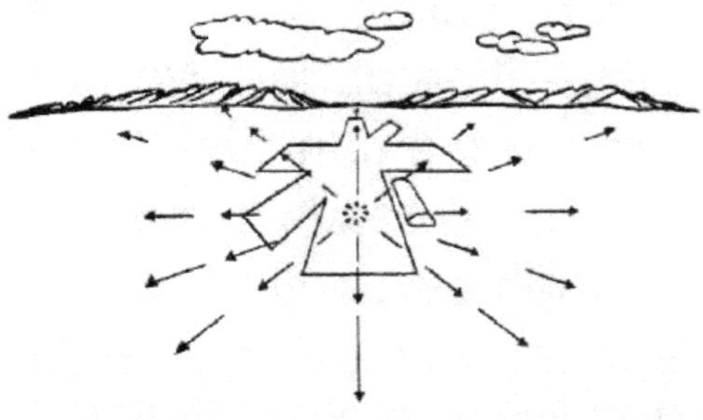

THE OPTIC ARRAY LANDING GUIDE

Optic Flow Patterns

- If there are no changes or flow in the optic array, the perceiver is static. If there are changes or flow, then the perceiver is moving.
- The flow either comes from a specific point or moves to a specific point. The perceiver can tell which direction they are moving based on the center of the movement; if flow is moving towards the specific point, then the perceiver is moving farther away from it, but if the flow is coming out from the specific point, then the perceiver is moving towards it.

Invariants

Every time we move our eyes, head, or walk around, things start to shift in and out of our viewing field. For this reason, it is rare that we see a stagnant view of objects or scenes.

- As you approach an object, the texture will expand, and as you move farther away from an object, the texture will contract.

- Because the flow of texture occurs the same way when moving around, it is known as invariant. This provides information about our environment and is an essential cue to showing depth.
- Texture and linear perspective are two good examples of invariants.

Affordances

Affordances are environmental cues that support perception and provide meaning. Gibson didn't believe that long-term memory provided meanings, but instead thought an object's potential use was directly perceivable. For example, a chair provides for the chance to sit and a ladder provides for the chance to climb up or down. Important affordances include:

Texture Gradient giving the appearance of depth.

TEXTURE AS A MEANS TO SHOW DEPTH

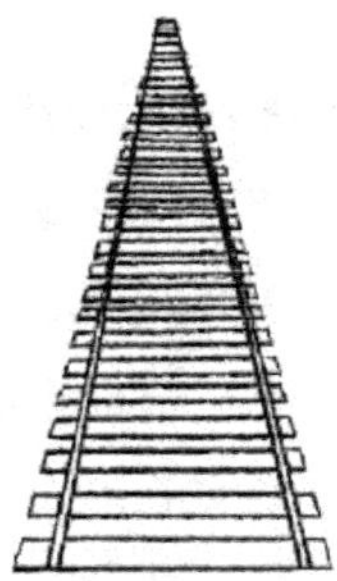

Parallel Lines, eg railway tracks, appear to converge as they recede into the distance

LINEAR PERSPECTIVE EXAMPLE

- **Optical array:** The patterns of light from the environment that reach the eye.
- **Relative brightness:** Objects that feature clearer and brighter

images are perceived as being closer.

- **Relative size:** As an object moves away, the image seen by the eye appears smaller, and objects that have smaller images are seen as being farther away.
- **Height in the visual field:** When an object is farther away, this means that it is usually higher in the visual field.
- **Texture gradient:** When an object moves away, the grain of texture will become smaller.
- **Superimposition:** When an image of one object is blocking another object's image from being seen, this means the first object is viewed as being closer than the second object.

Neither Gregory's nor Gibson's theories are able to accurately describe all of perception, and there have been additional theories put forth that claim top-down processes and bottom-up processes interact with one another to create the best interpretation. Regardless of the final solution, both interpretations of perception have paved the way for psychologists' consideration of this difficult issue.

GESTALT PSYCHOLOGY

Looking at behavior and the mind as a whole

Created by Max Wertheimer, Kurt Koffka, and Wolfgang Kohler in the 1920s, Gestalt psychology is a school of thought based on the notion that behavior and the intricacies of the mind should not be studied separately but looked at as a whole, because this is often how humans experience events.

Gestalt psychology claims that the whole is not simply the same as the sum of its parts. Through this notion, Gestalt psychologists were able to break down perceptual organization into a series of principles and explain how small objects can group together to create larger objects. Using this same idea, Gestalt therapy looks at behavior, speech, and how an individual experiences the world around him or her in order to help the individual become whole, or more aware.

GESTALT PRINCIPLES OF PERCEPTUAL ORGANIZATION

In trying to express the notion that the whole is not the same as the sum of its parts, Gestalt psychologists created a series of principles, known as the Gestalt principles of perceptual organization. These principles, which are actually mental shortcuts that people perform in order to solve a problem, successfully explain how objects that are smaller can group together and become objects that are larger, and show that there is a difference between the whole and the various parts that make up the whole.

THE LAW OF SIMILARITY

People tend to group together items that are similar. In the following image, people usually see vertical columns made up of circles and squares.

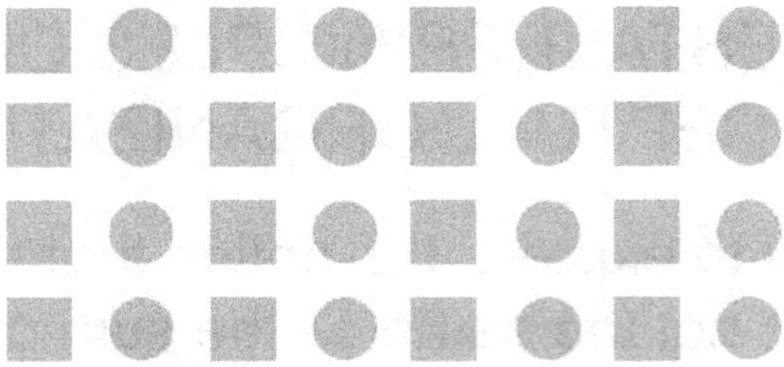

PERCEIVED SIMILAR GROUPINGS

THE LAW OF PRAGNANZ

In German, “pragnanz” means “good figure.” The law of pragnanz states we view objects in their simplest possible form.

For example, in the following image, instead of seeing a series of complex shapes, we see five circles.

SIMPLIFIED PERCEIVED GROUPINGS

THE LAW OF PROXIMITY

The law of proximity states that when objects are near one another, people have the tendency to group them together.

In the following image, the circles on the right appear as if they are grouped together in horizontal rows, while the circles on the left appear as if they are grouped together in vertical columns.

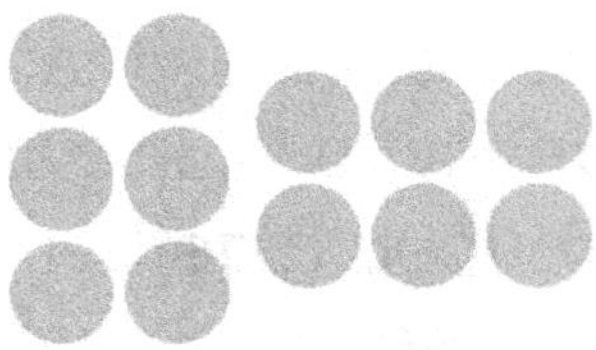

PROXIMAL GROUPINGS

THE LAW OF CONTINUITY

The law of continuity states that people will find the smoothest path when points seem connected by curving or straight lines. These lines will appear as if they belong with one another, instead of appearing as individual lines and angles.

For example, in the following image, instead of viewing the bottom part as a separate line, we view it as an extension of the series.

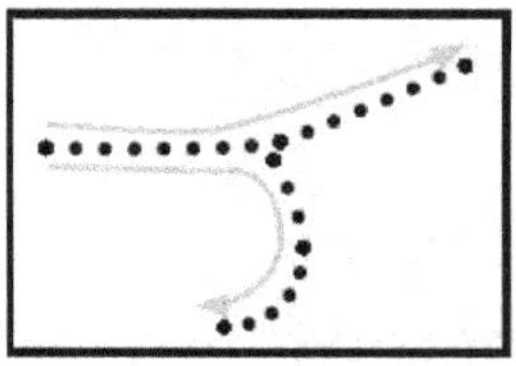

PERCEIVED SMOOTH TRANSITIONS

THE LAW OF CLOSURE

The law of closure states that our brains have the tendency to fill in gaps when objects are grouped together so that the grouping can be seen as a whole.

In the following image, for example, the gaps between the objects are ignored by our brains, and we complete the contour lines. Our brains fill in this missing information and create triangles and circles—shapes that are familiar to us.

PERCEIVING SHAPES IN NEGATIVE SPACE

FIGURE-GROUND

Figure-ground shows that people have an innate tendency to recognize only one part of an event as the figure (also known as foreground) and the other as the background. Even though this is a single image, either a vase or two faces can be seen, but never at the same time.

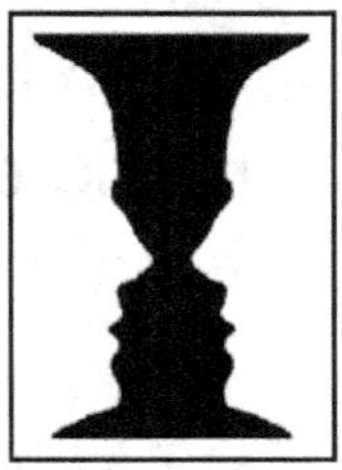

FOREGROUND AND BACKGROUND RECOGNITION

GESTALT THERAPY

Drawing upon the work of early Gestalt perceptual psychology, as well as several other influences such as the work of Sigmund Freud, Karen Horney, and even the theatre, husband and wife Frederick and Laura Perls created Gestalt therapy in the 1940s.

Much like Gestalt psychology focused on the whole, Gestalt therapy focuses on the whole being of a person through items such as behavior, speech, posture, and how an individual encounters the world.

Whereas early Gestalt psychology focused on foreground and background in the figure-ground theory, Gestalt therapy uses the idea of foreground and background to help an individual become self-aware. It helps them identify who they are in a background of situations and emotions that remain unresolved.

COMMON GESTALT THERAPY TECHNIQUES

A common technique used in Gestalt therapy is that of role-playing. This helps an individual work out a resolution to an otherwise unfinished situation or problem. The most common role-playing technique used is the "empty chair technique," where a person will talk to an empty chair as if someone were sitting in it. This technique not only allows one to vent, but also helps a person find new ways to solve their problems.

Gestalt therapy also places great emphasis on dream analysis, believing that dreams can bring out the psychology of an individual as well as any trauma from the individual's past. A technique commonly used in Gestalt therapy is to have an individual write their dreams down for two weeks, choose one that feels particularly important or significant, and actually act it out. This allows a person to reconnect with parts of their experience that have since been disowned.

Another common technique used in Gestalt therapy is hitting a sofa with soft bats or padded sticks to release feelings of anger. By visualizing what you are angry about and hitting it with the bats or sticks, you can release unproductive anger and move on to focusing on your true self.

Lastly, one of the most famous Gestalt therapy techniques is also one of the simplest. Because the idea behind Gestalt therapy is to become self-aware, one must first increase their awareness. This can be done by saying "I am aware that ... " and defining oneself in that way.

You can say, “I am aware that I am sitting at my desk,” “I am aware that I feel sad right now,” and so on. This technique helps keep a person in the present, separates feelings from interpretations and judgments, and helps produce a clearer vision of how that person understands himself or herself to be.

COGNITIVE PSYCHOLOGY

Understanding what's really going on in your head

Cognitive psychology is the branch of psychology that focuses on how a person acquires, processes, and stores information. Prior to the 1950s, the dominant school of thought had been behaviorism. For the next twenty years, the psychology world began to shift away from studying observable behaviors and moved towards studying internal mental processes, focusing on topics such as attention, memory, problem solving, perception, intelligence, decision making, and language processing. Cognitive psychology differed from psychoanalysis because it used scientific research methods to learn about mental processes, instead of simply relying on the subjective perceptions of a psychoanalyst.

The 1950s through the 1970s is now commonly referred to as the "cognitive revolution" because it was during this time period that processing models and research methods were created. American psychologist Ulric Neisser first used the term in his 1967 book, *Cognitive Psychology*.

The Two Assumptions of Cognitive Psychology

Individual parts of mental processes can be recognized and understood by scientific method, and one can describe internal mental processes with algorithms or rules in information processing models.

ATTENTION

In cognitive psychology, attention refers to how an individual actively processes information specifically present in his or her environment. When you read this book, you are also experiencing the numerous sights, sounds, and sensations around you: the weight of the book in your hands, the sounds of the person next to you talking on the phone, the feeling of sitting on your chair, the sight of the trees outside your window, the memory of a previous conversation you had, and more. Psychologists that study cognitive psychology want to understand how a person can experience all of these different sensations and still focus on just a single element or task.

FOUR TYPES OF ATTENTION

- **Focused attention:** A short-term response, which can be as short as eight seconds, to very specific auditory, tactile, or visual stimuli. For example, a phone ringing or a sudden occurrence might cause someone to focus on it for a few seconds, but then they will turn back to the task they were performing or think about something unrelated to the ringing phone.

- **Sustained attention:** A level of attention that will produce consistent results involving a task performed over time that is continuous and repetitive. For example, if a person washing dishes shows sustained attention, they will perform the task until completed. If a person loses focus, they may stop halfway through and move on to another task. Most adults and teenagers cannot show sustained attention on one task for more than twenty minutes, and will instead repeatedly choose to refocus on the task, which enables them to pay attention to things that are longer, like movies.
- **Divided attention:** Paying attention to several things at a single time. This is a limited ability, and it impacts how much information gets processed.
- **Selective attention:** Paying attention to specific things while filtering out others. For example, if you are at a loud party, you are still

able to maintain a conversation with someone even though there are other sensations going on around you.

INATTENTIONAL BLINDNESS AND THE INVISIBLE GORILLA TEST

Inattentional blindness shows what happens when a person is overloaded with sensations. This takes place when a person does not notice obvious stimuli, even though they are right in front of the person. Inattentional blindness happens to everyone because it is mentally and physically impossible to notice every stimulus. One of the most famous experiments showcasing inattentional blindness is Daniel Simon's Invisible Gorilla Test.

A group of subjects were asked to watch a short video of two groups of people (one group wearing white T-shirts, the other black T-shirts) as two basketballs were passed around within their respective groups. The subjects were asked to count how many times the basketball was passed in one group.

Meanwhile, as the two groups passed their basketballs to each other, a person in a gorilla suit walked to the center, beat his chest, and then walked off screen.

When the video was over, the test subjects were asked if they noticed anything unusual, and in most cases, 50 percent had not seen the gorilla. This experiment demonstrates that attention plays a significant role in the relationship between a person's perception and visual field.

PROBLEM SOLVING

In cognitive psychology, a problem is defined as a question or situation that involves difficulty, uncertainty, or doubt. The mental process of problem solving consists of discovery, analysis, and solving the problem, with the ultimate goal being to overcome an obstacle and resolve the issue with the best possible solution.

The Problem-Solving Cycle

Researchers believe that the best way to solve a problem is through a series of steps known as the problem-solving cycle. It is important to note, however, that even though the steps are listed sequentially, people rarely follow this series of steps rigidly and will instead skip various steps or go back as many times as needed until they have reached a desired result.

1. **Identify the Problem:** It is in this first step that the existence of a problem is first recognized. Though it sounds simple enough, mistakenly identifying the source of the problem will render any attempts to solve it inefficient and possibly useless.
2. **Define the Problem and Identify Limitations:** Once the existence of a problem has been identified, a person must fully define what his or her problem is in order for it to be solved. In other words, now that there is an acknowledgment of a problem's

existence, the definition of what the problem actually is becomes clearer.

3. **Form a Solution Strategy:** The approach to creating a strategy will depend on the situation and the unique preferences of the individual.
4. **Organize Information about the Problem:** A person must now organize any available information so he or she can be prepared to come up with a fitting solution.
5. **Allocate and Use the Mental and Physical Resources Needed:** Depending on the importance of the problem, it might be necessary to allocate certain resources of money, time, or something else. If the problem is not as important, using too many resources may not be essential to coming up with a solution.
6. **Monitor Progress:** If no progress is being made, then it is

time to reevaluate the approach and search for different strategies.

7. **Evaluate the Results for Accuracy:** To make sure the solution was the absolute best outcome, the results must be evaluated. This can either be done over time, such as evaluating the results of a workout regimen; or it can be immediately, such as checking the answer to a math problem.

COGNITIVE STRATEGIES FOR PROBLEM SOLVING

There are two types of problems: well-defined problems and ill-defined problems. Problems that are well-defined have goals that are clear, feature a very specific path leading to a solution, and have obstacles that are easy to identify based on the provided information. Problems that are ill-defined do not feature a specific path or formula leading to a solution and need to be investigated so that the problem can be defined, understood, and solved.

Because using a formula cannot solve ill-defined problems, information must be collected and analyzed to come up with a solution. Ill-defined problems can also feature well-defined sub-problems. In order to find a solution, a combination of problem-solving strategies may be required. Researchers have reportedly found more than fifty different strategies for problem solving. Some of the most common include:

- **Brainstorm:** List every option without evaluating them, analyze the options, and then choose one.
- **Analogy:** Use an option that has been learned from similar problems.
- **Break down:** Take a problem that is large or complex and break it down into problems that are smaller and simpler.
- **Hypothesis testing:** Create a hypothesis based on the cause of the problem, gather information, and test it.

- **Trial and error:** Test random solutions until you have found the right one.
- **Research:** Adapt and use existing ideas for problems that are similar.
- **Means/Ends analysis:** At each phase of the problem-solving cycle, take an action to get closer to the goal.

MEMORY

Memory in cognitive psychology refers to the processes used in acquiring, storing, retaining, and retrieving information. There are three main processes: encoding, storage, and retrieval.

To create a new memory, information must first go through encoding so it can be transformed into a useable form. Following encoding, the information is stored in our memory so that it can be used later. Most of our stored memory is actually outside of our awareness until it is needed. When it is needed, this information goes through the retrieval process, allowing for stored memory to be brought into our conscious awareness.

To understand the basic function and structure of memory, one can look at the stage model of memory, which proposes three separate stages:

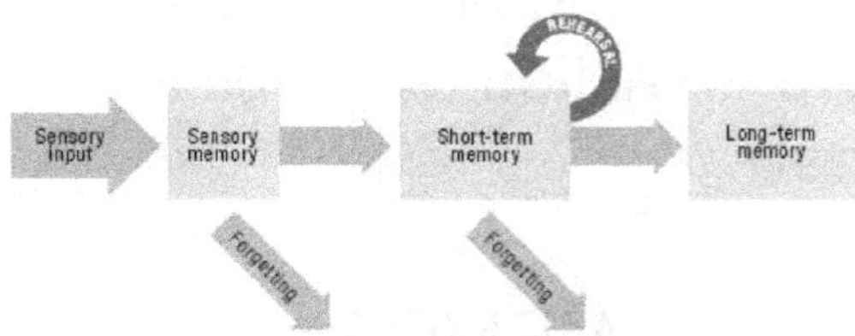

PROGRESSION OF MEMORY FORMATION

1. **Sensory Memory:** This is the earliest stage in the memory process. Sensory information that has been gathered from the environment as an exact copy of what is seen or heard is stored for a short period of time. Auditory information is stored for three to four seconds, while visual information is usually stored for no longer than half of a second. Only particular aspects of the sensory memory are attended to, and this

allows some information to move on to the next stage.

2. **Short-Term Memory:** Also known as active memory, this is the information that we are currently thinking about or aware of. This information will be kept for twenty to thirty seconds, and it is generated by paying attention to sensory memories. Though short-term memories are often quickly forgotten, if this information is attended to by repetition, it will move on to the next stage.
3. **Long-Term Memory:** This is the continuous storage of information. Freud would refer to long-term memory as the unconscious and preconscious. The information here is outside of a person's awareness but can be called upon and used when needed. While some information will be easy to recollect, other information can be much more difficult to access.

The Differences Between Short-Term Memory and Long-Term Memory

The differences between short-term memory and long-term memory become very clear when discussing memory retrieval. Short-term memory is stored and recollected in sequential order and is mostly comprised of sensory memories. So for example, if you were told a list of words and were asked to recall the sixth word, you would have to list the words in the order you heard them to get the right information. Long-term memory, however, is stored and recalled based on meaning and association.

HOW MEMORY IS ORGANIZED

Because we can access and recollect information from long-term memory, a person can then use these memories when interacting with others, making decisions, and problem solving. But how the information is organized still remains a mystery. What we do know, however, is that memories are arranged in groups through a process known as clustering.

In clustering, information is categorized so that it becomes easier to recall. For example, take a look at the following group of words:

Green
Table
Raspberry
Blue
Desk
Banana
Peach
Magenta
Bureau

If you were to read this list, look away, and then try to write down the words, your memory would likely group the words into different categories: colors, fruits, and furniture.

Tip of the Tongue?

Research suggests that the more time spent trying to figure out the word you were going to say actually increases the chances that you'll struggle with that word again later on.

Memory plays an extremely large role in our lives. From the short-term to the long-term, our experiences and our way of looking at the world are shaped by our memory. And even with all that we do understand about the subject, what memory truly is, at its most basic level, still remains a mystery.

COGNITIVE DISSONANCE THEORY

Fighting yourself

In 1957, psychologist Leon Festinger suggested in his cognitive dissonance theory that every person has an inner drive and desire to avoid dissonance (or disharmony) in all of their attitudes and beliefs (cognitions), and that they ultimately wish to achieve harmony (consonance) among their cognitions.

If a person has feelings of discomfort due to conflicting, simultaneous cognitions, this is known as cognitive dissonance. In order to reduce the discomfort and restore balance, a cognition has to undergo an alteration of some sort.

Festinger began investigating his theory while studying participants from a cult. The people he observed believed that the planet was going to be destroyed by a great flood, and some members went to extreme lengths for the cause they believed in, selling their homes and leaving their jobs in anticipation of the coming calamity. When the great flood they had spoken of never occurred, Festinger wanted to observe their reactions.

While some recognized that they had been foolish and left the cult, members that were more committed to the cause reinterpreted evidence to support their story, claiming that the earth was saved because of the cult members' faithfulness.

When the cognitions were inconsistent, the members of the cult sought to alter their beliefs to restore consistency and harmony.

Doctoral Definition

Cognition: A part of knowledge in the form of an emotion, behavior, idea, belief, value, or attitude. For example, the knowledge that you caught a baseball, the knowledge that a song makes you happy, and the knowledge that you like the color green are all cognitions. A person can have many cognitions going on concurrently, and cognitions will create dissonant and consonant relationships with other cognitions.

THE COGNITIVE DISSONANCE EXPERIMENT

Dissonance can be created when a person is forced to do something in public that in private they would not want to do. This creates a dissonance between the cognition, which states, "I did not want to do that," and the behavior. This is also known as forced compliance, which occurs when a person does something that is inconsistent with what he or she believes.

Because a past behavior cannot be changed, the only way to reduce the dissonance is by re-evaluating and changing the person's attitude towards the behavior. To prove forced compliance, Leon Festinger and James Carlsmith conducted the following experiment.

EXPERMIENT

COGNITIVE DISSONANCE BOREDOM EXPERIMENT

1. Divide your test subjects into two groups: Group A and Group B. Group A should not be provided any introduction about the tasks, and Group B should be given an introduction that presents the activities in an enjoyable and interesting manner.
2. Start out by having the participants perform a series of incredibly boring and repetitive tasks. For the first half hour, ask the subjects to place twelve spools on and off of a tray with one hand. For the next half hour, have the subjects turn square pegs clockwise on a pegboard in quarter-turns, again only using one hand. Once the cycle has been finished and all forty-eight square pegs are turned the subjects will have to start turning the square pegs again.

3. Once completed, interview the subjects on how enjoyable they found the tasks to be.
4. Let around one-third of the subjects go at this point. This is your control group. Prior to being released, these people should discuss in their interview how the project could be improved for future studies.
5. Everyone else remaining will be given the option of becoming the experimenter. All they have to do is tell the next group of participants about the tasks they are about to perform in a positive manner. Half of the group will be offered $1 for their contribution, and the other half will be offered $20 for their contribution.
6. Interview the subjects once again and ask them to rate these four parts of the experiment: whether they feel the tasks they had to perform were enjoyable or interesting (on a scale of -5 to +5); whether this experiment allows them to learn about their own skills

(on a scale of 0 to 10); whether they believe this experiment was measuring anything important (on a scale of 0 to 10); and whether the participant would want to do another study like this in the future (on a scale of -5 to +5).

The Results

In Festinger and Carlsmith's original experiment, eleven of the seventy-one responses were deemed invalid for a variety of reasons. Of the remaining responses, the scores were as reported below:

INTERVIEW QUESTION	EXPERIMENTAL CONDITION CONTROL (N=20)	EXPERIMENTAL CONDITION ONE DOLLAR (N=20)	EXPERIMENTAL CONDITION TWENTY DOLLARS (N=20)
How enjoyable the tasks were (from -5 to +5)	-.45	+1.35	-.05
How much you learned (from 0 to 10)	3.08	2.80	3.15
Scientific importance (from 0 to 10)	5.60	6.45	5.18
Would you participate in a similar experiment (from -5 to +5)	-.62	1.20	-.25

Festinger and Carlsmith believed the answer to the first question was the most important and that these results showed cognitive dissonance. Because the control group was not offered any money, this was how the participants truly felt about the test (rating it a negative 0.45). The dramatic difference between the group that was offered $1 and the group that was offered $20 can be explained by cognitive dissonance.

The subjects involved in the study were conflicted between the cognitions “I told someone the test was interesting” and “I really found it to be boring.” When offered a single dollar, the participants began internalizing and rationalizing their attitudes into thinking that it was actually enjoyable because there was no other justification to be had. Festinger and Carlsmith believed that the group that was offered $20, however, had the money as a justification for their actions. Therefore, the group that was offered $1 had insufficient justification for their actions and experienced cognitive dissonance.

DRIVE REDUCTION THEORY

Trying to balance yourself out

In the 1940s and 1950s, behaviorist Clark Hull set out to explain behavior with his drive reduction theory. Essentially, Hull believed that all people have biological needs—which he referred to as "drives"—that motivate our behaviors and create unpleasant states. Hull believed that these drives were internal states of tension or arousal that were physiological or biological in nature. The primary influence of motivation came from the desire to reduce these drives, which Hull believed was critical in order to maintain an internal calm. Common examples of drives in Hull's conception include thirst, hunger, and the need to be warm. To reduce these drives, we drink liquids, eat food, and put on extra clothing or turn up the heat on our thermostats.

Drawing on the works of Ivan Pavlov, Charles Darwin, and John B. Watson, among others, Hull based the drive reduction theory on the notion of homeostasis, believing that behavior was one method of maintaining balance.

Doctoral Definition

Homeostasis: The idea that the body needs to reach a level of equilibrium, or balance, and then maintain that state. For example, the way the body regulates body temperature.

Hull was considered a neo-behaviorist and believed that behavior could be explained with conditioning and reinforcement. A behavior is reinforced by the reduction of a drive, and this reinforcement will increase the chances of that behavior occurring again, should the need arise in the future.

THE MATHEMATICO-DEDUCTIVE THEORY OF BEHAVIOR

Along with the theory of drive reduction, Hull attempted to create a formula of learning and behavior that could empirically accompany his theories and offer a deeper and more technical understanding of how drives influence action and thought. His resulting equation, known as the Mathematico-Deductive Theory of Behavior, is:

$$sEr = V \times D \times K \times J \times sHr - sIr - Ir - sOr - sLr$$

sEr: This stands for excitatory potential, meaning the chance that an organism will create a response (r) to a stimulus (s)
V: The stimulus
D: The strength of the drive, determined by the amount of biological deprivation
K: The size of the goal, known as the incentive motivation
J: The delay before reinforcement can be sought
sHr: The strength of the habit, as determined by the amount of conditioning that occurred previously
sIr: This is known as the conditioned inhibition, and it is the result of a previous

absence or lack of reinforcement
Ir: This is the reaction inhibition, otherwise known as lethargy or fatigue
sOr: An allowance for error that is random
sLr: This is the reaction threshold, or the lowest amount of reinforcement needed to create learning

CRITICISMS OF THE DRIVE REDUCTION THEORY

While Hull's work on the scientific method and experimental techniques left a profound impact on the world of psychology, his drive reduction theory is largely ignored today. As a result of the narrowly defined variables in his accompanying formula, his theory makes it difficult to create predictions based on recurring experiences.

One of the largest issues with Hull's drive reduction theory is that it does not take into account the role of secondary reinforcers and how they play a part in reducing drive. Where primary reinforcers deal with drives that are biological or physiological in nature, secondary reinforcers do not reduce these biological or physiological needs in a direct manner. Money, for example, is a secondary reinforcer. Money cannot reduce a drive; however it is a source of reinforcement, and can allow one to obtain a primary reinforcer to reduce a drive.

Another criticism of Hull's drive reduction theory is that there is no explanation as to why a person will engage in certain behaviors that do not actually reduce drives. Why would a person drink if they are not thirsty? Why would they eat if they are not hungry? Some people will even increase tension by participating in activities like bungee jumping and skydiving. These activities do not fulfill any sort of biological need and even place the participant in danger. Ultimately, though it is a flawed theory, Hull's work on drive reduction spurred a generation of psychologists to attempt a deeper understanding of the precise factors that cause humans to act and react in their environments.

HARRY HARLOW (1905–1981)

He wasn't just monkeying around

Harry Harlow (née Harry Israel) was born on October 31st, 1905, in Fairfield, Iowa. Originally, Israel attended Reed College in Oregon, but transferred to Stanford University with hopes to major in English. In 1930, now going by the last name Harlow, Harry graduated from Stanford University with a BA and PhD in psychology.

Following graduation, Harlow began to teach at the University of Wisconsin-Madison, and within a year, he created the Psychology Primate Lab, which merged with the Wisconsin Regional Primate Lab in 1964. Harlow became director of the research center, where he would conduct many of his most significant and controversial experiments.

Harlow's work focused on love, and he questioned the then-popular theory of attachment, which claimed that love was derived from a mother's feeding and then applied to other members of the family by extension.

In 1957, Harlow began his now famous —and infamous—work with rhesus monkeys to show the effects of love. This research would not only leave a tremendous impact on the world of psychology, but it also played a key role in changing the approaches taken by childcare facilities like orphanages, social service groups, adoption agencies, and childcare providers when it came to caring for children.

Though Harlow studied love, his own endeavors in love were rather complicated. He married his first wife (who had been a student of his) in 1932. He and his wife had two children together, and they got divorced in 1946. That same year, Harlow got married to a child psychologist who he would have another two children with. Harlow's second wife died in 1970, after a long battle with cancer; and in 1971, Harlow actually remarried his first wife. Following the death of his second wife, Harlow battled depression and alcoholism and became estranged from his children. Harry Harlow died on December 6th, 1981.

The Many Accolades of Harry Harlow

Harry Harlow received many honors and awards during his life, including:

- Head of the Human Resources Research Branch of the Department of the Army (1950–1952)
- Head of the Division of Anthropology and Psychology of the National Research Council (1952–1955)
- The Howard Crosby Warren Medal (1956)
- President of the American Psychological Association (1958–1959)
- The National Medal of Science (1967)

- The Gold Medal from the American Psychological Foundation (1973)

THE RHESUS MONKEY EXPERIMENTS

Harlow disagreed with the notion that the initial relationship between a mother and child was simply based on relieving thirst, obtaining food, and avoiding pain. Using baby rhesus monkeys, he created experiments to attempt to describe and categorize love. Baby rhesus monkeys are actually more mature than human babies; and similar to their human counterparts, they can express a range of emotions and have to be nursed.

In one of Harlow's most famous experiments, he created two "mothers" for the baby rhesus monkeys to choose from. He took the young monkeys from their mothers only a few hours after having been born and immediately placed them with the two artificial mothers. One “mother” was made up of soft terrycloth but had no food for the baby monkeys, and the other “mother” was composed of wire and had a bottle with food attached to it.

Harlow observed that the baby monkeys only spent as much time as necessary with the wireframe mother in order to get a sufficient amount of food, and would not stay any longer, but enjoyed spending time and cuddling with the terrycloth mother. His results proved that the monkeys were not simply following their physiological needs, and that the bond between mother and infant could not be simplified to only the result of nursing.

Harlow then separated the monkeys into two groups: one group was to only spend time with the terrycloth mother, and the other was to only spend time with the wireframe mother. In both groups, the monkeys drank the same amount and grew at the same rate. However, there were major differences between the behaviors of the two groups, which Harlow explained as the result of an emotional attachment the monkeys with the terrycloth mother had that the monkeys with the wireframe mother did not.

When objects and noises frightened the monkeys with the terrycloth mother, they would run to the mother for security and make contact with it until they were calm. When the monkeys with the wireframe mother were frightened, however, they dropped to the floor, rocked back and forth, held themselves, and screamed. These latter behaviors, Harlow noted, resembled those of autistic children, and mirrored the actions of adults who had been confined in mental institutions.

Harlow followed up these experiments with even more inhumane practices. In an effort to see if "better late than never" proved true, Harlow put baby rhesus monkeys in complete isolation for the first eight months of their lives. This meant no contact with other monkeys or any type of surrogate mother. These tests left the monkeys with significant emotional damage. After testing various lengths of time that monkeys could go motherless, Harlow concluded that maternal deprivation could in fact be reversed, but only if it lasted for less than ninety days for the monkeys, or up to six months for humans.

THE IMPACT OF HARLOW'S WORK

While his work was controversial and would be deemed inhumane by today's standards, Harry Harlow's work was extremely important and left a dramatic impact on child rearing, childcare, adoption agencies, orphanages, and social services.

Harlow was able to show with irrefutable evidence that love was vital in the development of a normal child and that deprivation could lead to severe emotional damage. His work was instrumental in the development of treatments for abused and neglected children, and it also showed that when it came to the emotional and mental well-being of a child, adoption was a far superior option to institutional childcare.

JEAN PIAGET (1896–1980)

The development of children

Jean Piaget was born on August 9th, 1896, in Neuchâtel, Switzerland, to a professor of medieval literature and a mother Piaget would later recall as neurotic, whose behavior would eventually stoke his interest in the field of psychology.

Following high school, Piaget received his PhD in natural sciences from the University of Neuchâtel. While spending a semester at the University of Zurich, he became very interested in psychoanalysis and soon moved to France. It was while working at a boys' institution created by Alfred Binet that he began performing experimental studies on the developing mind. Prior to Piaget's work in cognitive development, the common belief was that adults were simply more competent thinkers than children. While working at the Binet Institute, Piaget became interested in the reasons children provided him when they answered logical-thinking questions incorrectly. Piaget then set out to create a systematic study of cognitive development, and would become the first to do so.

In 1923, Jean Piaget married Valentine Châtenay, and they would have three children together. Piaget—who was already fascinated by mental and emotional growth—began informally studying the development of his children. These observations would lead to some of his most important and renowned work: the stages of cognitive development.

With more than sixty books and several hundred articles published, Jean Piaget left his mark not only in the field of psychology, but also in education, sociology, economics, law, and epistemology. Jean Piaget died on September 16th, 1980.

PIAGET'S THEORY OF COGNITIVE DEVELOPMENT

When Piaget began working on his theory of cognitive development, there were some very big differences between what he was doing and what had been done in the past.

- Rather than concentrating on all learners, Piaget focused on children.
- Piaget's theory did not discuss the learning of a specific behavior or the learning of information, but rather his theory looked at overall development.
- Instead of the common notion that cognitive development was gradual and the amount of behaviors grew and became more complex, Piaget proposed a series of discrete stages that were evident by qualitative differences.

Piaget believed that instead of being less competent than adults, children are actually born with a basic mental structure that is the result of genetics and evolution, and that this structure is what knowledge and learning is derived from. From this assumption, Piaget attempted to explain the processes and mechanisms infants and children develop that eventually lead them to think with reason and with the use of hypotheses. Piaget believed that children create an understanding of their environment and experience discrepancies between what is already known and what will be discovered. His theory of cognitive development can be broken down into three different components:

1. **Schemas:** Schemas are the basic building blocks, or units, of knowledge. Each schema relates to one part of the world, such as actions, objects, and concepts. Each schema is a series of linked representations of the world that are used to understand and respond to a particular situation. For example, if a parent shows their child a picture of a dog, the child will create a schema of what

a dog looks like: it has four legs, a tail, and ears.

If a child can explain what he or she perceives with existing schemas, this is known as being in a state of equilibrium, or mental balance.

Schemas are stored so that they can be applied later on. For example, a child might form a schema about how to order food at a restaurant, and so the next time that child is at a restaurant, he or she will be able to apply what he or she has learned to this new and similar situation.

Piaget also claimed that some schemas are genetically programmed into children, such as a baby's impulse to suck on things.

2. **Processes that allow one stage to transition into another:** Piaget believed intellectual growth was the result of adaptation and the need to always be in a state of equilibrium. Adaptation of knowledge occurs in two ways:

- **Assimilation:** Using a schema that already exists and applying it to a new situation.
- **Accommodation:** Changing an existing schema to take in new information.

To better understand how assimilation and accommodation work, we can look at the earlier situation of the parent showing their child what a dog looks like. The child now has a schema of what a dog is: four legs, a tail, ears, etc. When the child is approached by an actual dog, the child now faces new characteristics that were not originally part of their schema. The dog is furry; the dog licks; the dog can bark. Because these were not in the original schema, there is disequilibrium and the child begins to construct meaning. When the parent confirms that this information is also for a dog, assimilation occurs and equilibrium is regained as the child incorporates this information into the original schema.

But what if the child saw a cat? The cat has some similar features as a dog;

however, it is a different animal. It meows, has the ability to climb, and moves and acts differently from a dog. As a result of seeing the cat, the child is placed in disequilibrium and must accommodate this new information. A new schema is formed and the child returns to a state of equilibrium.

3. **The Stages of Development:** Piaget believed that cognition develops in four stages. These stages occur in every child and follow the same exact order, no matter the child's culture or the part of the world they live in; though, some children may never reach the later stages.

   - **Sensorimotor (birth–two years)**
     This stage focuses on object permanence, where a child comes to the realization that objects will continue to exist even if they are not seen or heard by the child.
   - **Preoperational (two–seven years)**
     This stage focuses on egocentrism,

meaning that from two to seven years old, children are not able to understand the point of view of others.

- **Concrete Operational (seven–eleven years)**
  This stage focuses on conservation, meaning that children are still not able to understand concepts that are abstract or hypothetical, but can begin thinking logically about concrete events.
- **Formal Operational (eleven years and older)**
  This stage focuses on the child's ability to manipulate ideas in their head, or think abstractly. It is during this stage that deductive reasoning, logical thought, and systematic planning emerge.

CRITIQUES OF PIAGET'S THEORY

The majority of criticism is based on Piaget's research methods. Not only did Piaget study his own three children, but the other children used in his study were of a higher socioeconomic status, meaning a wide sample of the population was not used, making the results hard to generalize. Some studies also disagree with Piaget's claim that children automatically move from stage to stage, and many psychologists believe environmental factors also play a key role.

Lastly, researchers believe that Piaget actually underestimated the abilities of children, and that children as young as four to five years old are much less egocentric than Piaget claimed and have a much more sophisticated understanding of their cognitive processes. Nonetheless, Piaget's hypothesis ushered in a new focus on the mechanisms of childhood intellectual development and served as an important building block of many of the theories that have come since—even those that rebut his conclusions.

ALBERT BANDURA

(1925–PRESENT)

Learning by observing others

Albert Bandura was born on December 4th, 1925, in the small town of Mundare, Canada. Bandura's father laid tracks for the trans-Canada railroad, and his mother worked at a general store in the town.

Bandura attended the only school in his town—it employed just two teachers—and as a result, Bandura had to take his own initiative when it came to education. Following high school, Bandura attended the University of British Columbia. While originally majoring in biological sciences, Bandura stumbled upon the subject of psychology through happenstance. Because he arrived at the university much earlier than his classes began, he decided to take "filler classes" to pass the time. After thumbing through a course catalogue one day, he ended up choosing a psychology course.

In 1949, Bandura graduated from the University of British Columbia in just three years, majoring in psychology, and went on to attend graduate school at the University of Iowa, where he would also get his PhD. After he earned his PhD in 1952, Bandura was offered a position at Stanford University, where he continues to teach today.

Bandura is most known for his social learning theory, which showed that not all behavior was lead by rewards or reinforcements, as behaviorism claimed to be the case. Instead, he offered an alternative and somewhat more nuanced view of the social pressures that contribute to learned behaviors—a more modern approach which is still valued.

SOCIAL LEARNING THEORY

One of the most influential learning theories in psychology, Albert Bandura's social learning theory of 1977 states that instead of acquired behavior being strictly a matter of rewards or reinforcements, it can be brought about through observational learning. He states that people grasp how to behave based on the behavior of the people around them.

People are surrounded by models that can be observed, be it a person's parents, peers, teachers, or even characters on a TV show. These models provide both masculine and feminine behaviors that can be observed or encoded, and then later imitated or copied. A person will be more likely to imitate a behavior of someone who he or she feels more similar to. Often, this means a person of the same sex. There are three main concepts to Bandura's social learning theory:

1. **A person can learn behavior through observation:** This can be from a live model (an actual person performing the behavior), a verbal model that provides instructions (an explanation or description of a particular behavior), or a symbolic model (behaviors portrayed in books, television, and film).

2. **The mental state is an important aspect to learning:** While environmental reinforcement is one aspect of learning a behavior, it is not the only one. Satisfaction, pride, and feelings of accomplishment are examples of what Bandura called intrinsic or internal reinforcement. In other words, internal thoughts can play an important role in learning a behavior.
3. **Learning does not mean that a behavior will necessarily change:** Behaviorists believed that learning a behavior led to a permanent change in the individual's behavior, but Bandura shows that with observational learning, a person can learn the new information without having to demonstrate this behavior. Conversely, just because a behavior is observed does not mean it will be learned. For social learning to be a success, there are certain requirements:

- **Attention:** To learn, one must pay attention, and anything that diminishes attention will negatively affect observational learning.
- **Retention:** One must be able to store the information, and then at a later time be able to pull it back up and use it.
- **Reproduction:** After paying attention and retaining information, the observed behavior has to be performed. Practice can lead to improvement of the behavior.
- **Motivation:** The last part to successfully learning an observed behavior is that a person must be motivated to imitate the behavior. It is here where reinforcement and punishment come into play. If an observed behavior is reinforced, one might wish to duplicate that response; while if an observed behavior is punished, one might be motivated to not do such an action.

THE BOBO DOLL EXPERIMENT

To show that children observe and imitate behaviors around them, Bandura created the famous Bobo doll experiment.

In conducting his experiment, Bandura found that children who watched the aggressive models generally imitated a good deal more of the responses toward the bobo doll than the children in the control or the children in the group who watched the nonaggressive models.

He also found that girls who watched the aggressive model expressed more verbally aggressive responses when the model was the woman, and more physically aggressive responses when the model was the man. The boys imitated physically aggressive acts more than the girls did, and they imitated the same-sex model more often than the girls did.

Through the Bobo doll experiment, Bandura was able to successfully show that the children learned a social behavior, in this case aggression, by watching the behavior of someone else. With the Bobo doll experiment, Bandura was able to disprove a key notion of behaviorism that stated that all behavior is the result of rewards and reinforcement.

EXPERMIENT

CONDUCTING THE BOBO DOLL EXPERIMENT

1. This experiment utilizes thirty-six boys and thirty-six girls ranging from three to six years old.
2. The control for the experiment is a sub-group of twelve boys and twelve girls.
3. The role models in the experiment are one adult man and one adult woman.
4. Twenty-four boys and girls are allowed to watch as the man or woman aggressively attack a toy called the "Bobo doll." Among other things, they hit it with a hammer and throw it in the air while screaming things like, "Pow, boom," and "Sock him in the nose."
5. Another group of twenty-four boys and girls are exposed to a model who is nonaggressive toward the Bobo doll.

6. Lastly, the control group is not exposed to any model.

CARL ROGERS (1902–1987)

Helping others help themselves

Carl Rogers was born on January 8th, 1902, in Oak Park, Illinois, to a strict Protestant family. As a teenager, he and his family moved to Glen Ellen, Illinois, where Rogers took an interest in agriculture. In 1919, Rogers started attending the University of Wisconsin, where he decided to major in agriculture. He would later change his major to history, and then once again to religion.

During his junior year at the University of Wisconsin, Rogers and ten others were chosen to participate in an international Christian youth conference in China for six months. From this trip, Rogers began to question his choice of career. Following graduation in 1924, he attended the Union Theological Seminary, but transferred to Teachers College, Columbia University, in 1926. It was while at Teachers College, Columbia

University, that Rogers took his first psychology courses.

After earning his PhD in psychology, Rogers worked at Ohio State University, the University of Chicago, and the University of Wisconsin. While working at the University of Wisconsin, Rogers developed one of his most significant contributions to the world of psychology: client-centered therapy. Believing that a client or patient was ultimately in charge of their happiness, Rogers changed the role of the therapist from a mere technician into someone that would be able to guide a client towards happiness. The therapist was to embody empathy, congruence, and positive regard. In addition to this, Rogers created his "self-theory," which provided a description of how a client viewed him or herself, and how therapy would be able to change this view.

Today, the work of Carl Rogers would be considered "humanistic psychology." His ideas of how psychology should work focused less on diagnosing and more on how a person could help him or herself, with the ultimate goal to become what

Rogers referred to as a “fully-functioning person.” Carl Rogers died on February 4th, 1987.

SELF-ACTUALIZATION

Carl Rogers rejected the claims of both behaviorism (which claimed behavior was the result of conditioning) and psychoanalysis (which focused on the unconscious and biological factors), instead theorizing that a person behaves in certain ways because of how he or she perceives a situation and that only people themselves can know how they perceive things.

Rogers believed that people have one basic motive, the propensity to self-actualize.

Doctoral Definitions

SELF-ACTUALIZATION: When a person fulfills their potential and becomes fully-functioning, achieving the highest level of "human-beingness."

IDEAL SELF: This is what a person would like to be. This includes goals and ambitions, and is always changing.

In its most basic form, self-actualization can be understood by using the metaphor of a flower. A flower is constrained to its environment, and only under the right conditions will it be able to grow to its full potential.

Of course, humans are much more complex than flowers. We develop according to our personalities. Carl Rogers posited that people were inherently good and creative, and only became destructive when external constraints or a poor self-concept superseded the valuing process. Rogers claimed that a person with high self-worth, who has come close to attaining their ideal self, would be able to face the challenges they encountered in life, accept unhappiness and failure, feel confident and positive about his or herself, and be open with others. In order to achieve high self-worth and a degree of self-actualization, Rogers felt one must be in a state of congruence.

CONGRUENCE

If someone's ideal self is similar to or consistent with their actual experience, then they are experiencing a state of congruence. When there is a difference between someone's ideal self and their actual experience, this is known as incongruence.

It is very rare for a person to experience a complete state of congruence; but, Rogers states, a person has a higher sense of worth and is more congruent when the self-image (how one sees oneself) approaches the ideal self that a person is striving for. Because people want to view themselves in ways that are compatible with their self-image, they may begin to use defense mechanisms like repression or denial to feel less threatened by feelings that might be considered undesirable.

Rogers also emphasized the importance of other people in our lives, believing that people need to feel that they are regarded positively by others, because everyone possesses an inherent wish to be respected, valued, loved, and treated with affection. Rogers broke his idea of positive regard into two types:

1. **Unconditional positive regard:** When people are loved and respected for who they are, especially by their parents, significant others, and therapist. This leaves a person unafraid to try new things and to make mistakes, even if the consequences of these mistakes are not good. When a person can self-actualize, he or she usually receives unconditional positive regard.
2. **Conditional positive regard:** When people receive positive regard not because they are loved and respected for who they are, but because they behave in ways others think are correct. For

example, when children get approval from their parents because they behave the way their parents want them to act. Someone who always seeks approval from others most likely experienced conditional positive regard when he or she was growing up.

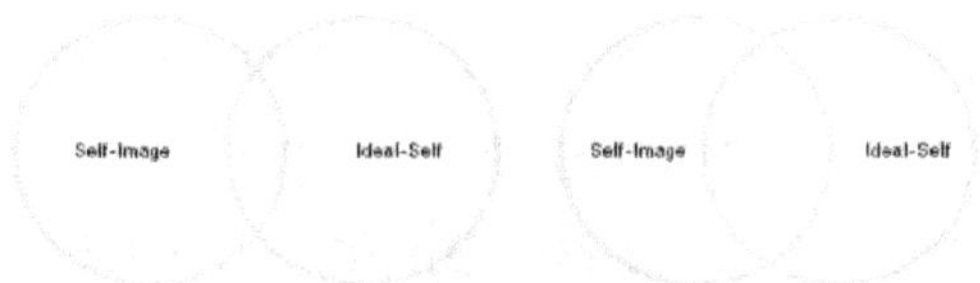

The self-image is different from the ideal self.
There is only a little overlap.
Here self-actualization will be difficult.

The self-image is similar to the ideal self.
There is more overlap.
This person can self-actualize.

VISUAL ILLUSTRATION OF CONGRUENCE

ABRAHAM MASLOW

(1908–1970)

Focusing on the human potential

Abraham Maslow was born on April 1st, 1908, in Brooklyn, New York. He was the oldest of seven children from Jewish Russian immigrants. Maslow later claimed that he was a shy child, lonely and unhappy, and recalled spending much of his youth at the library immersed in his studies.

Maslow began studying law at City College of New York, but soon transferred to the University of Wisconsin, where he began taking psychology courses. While there, Harry Harlow, famed for his rhesus monkey experiments, became Maslow's mentor and served as his doctoral adviser. Maslow attended the University of Wisconsin for all three of his psychology degrees, earning his bachelor's degree in 1930, his master's degree in 1931, and his PhD in 1934. Maslow then continued his psychology studies at Columbia University, where he found a further mentor in Alfred Adler, father of the inferiority complex.

In 1937, Maslow took a teaching position at Brooklyn College (where he would remain until 1951). While there, Maslow found two more mentors in Gestalt psychologist Max Wertheimer and anthropologist Ruth Benedict. Maslow admired these two people so much, both professionally and personally, that he began studying them and their behavior. This began Maslow's lifelong interest in human potential and mental health, and laid the groundwork for Maslow's most important contributions to psychology.

In the 1950s, Maslow became a founding father and leader of humanistic psychology. Instead of focusing on illness or the abnormal, Maslow focused on positive mental health. The founding of humanistic psychology led to the creation of several different types of therapy based on the notion that people have the potential to heal themselves through the use of therapy, and that the therapist was to act as a guide and help remove obstacles so that a patient could reach his or her potential.

Abraham Maslow is perhaps best known for his hierarchy of needs, a cornerstone of modern psychological thought and teaching, which suggests that people are motivated to fulfill a series of needs that start out as very basic and move to more advanced.

From 1951 to 1969, Maslow taught at Brandeis University, and in 1969, he moved to California to work at the Laughlin Institute. On June 8th, 1970, at the age of sixty-two, Abraham Maslow suffered from a heart attack and died.

HIERARCHY OF NEEDS

In 1943, Abraham Maslow first introduced the world to his hierarchy of needs, which is most often expressed as a pyramid. According to Maslow, needs play an important role in motivating a person to behave a certain way. The more basic a need is, the lower it is on the pyramid; and the more complex a need is, the higher it is on the pyramid. Needs towards the bottom of the pyramid are more physical, and needs towards the top become more psychological and social. In order to move up the pyramid, the levels must be completed from the bottom up. The needs are as follows:

Physiological

The physiological needs are the needs that are most basic and vital to survival. All other needs are secondary unless the needs in this category are met. These include the need for food, water, air, sleep, homeostasis, and sexual reproduction.

Safety

The safety and security needs are needs that are also important for survival, but are not as crucial as the physiological needs. This level of the model includes needs like personal security—such as a home and a safe neighborhood—financial security, health, and some form of safety net to protect against accidents, like insurance.

Love and Belonging

The love and belonging needs, also known as social needs, include a desire to belong, be loved, feel accepted, and not be lonely. These needs are less basic than the first two levels, and these needs can be met through friendships, romantic relationships, and family, as well as by being involved in religious, social, or community groups and organizations.

Esteem

Everyone has a need to be respected, valued by other people, and have a sense that they are contributing to the world. Having high self-esteem and the respect of others can lead to confidence, while low self-esteem and lack of respect from others can lead to feelings of inferiority. One way people can feel valued and have high self-esteem is by participating in professional activities, athletic teams, and hobbies, and through their academic accomplishments.

Self-Actualization

At the top of Maslow's model is the need for self-actualization, or the need to realize one's full potential. In other words, a person must become everything that they are capable of becoming. All other levels of Maslow's model must be completed before one can reach this level. While the need for self-actualization is broad, it is applied very specifically. For example, a person could desire to be the best possible painter, or to be an ideal father.

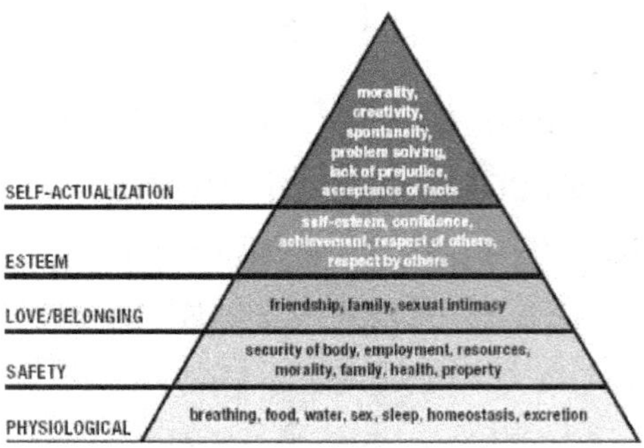

MASLOW'S HIERARCHY

Different Types of Needs

Maslow identified different varieties of needs, as well as different levels. Deficiency needs, or D-needs, are needs that arise out of deprivation (such as security needs, social needs, esteem needs, and physiological needs). These needs are lower-level needs, and must be satisfied in order to avoid feelings or consequences that are unpleasant. Growth needs, also known as Being-needs or B-needs, are needs that arise out of a desire to grow as a human being. Growth needs are not the result of deprivation.

CRITICISMS OF MASLOW'S HIERARCHY OF NEEDS

Maslow's hierarchy of needs has met its fair share of criticism. Most importantly, the method in which Maslow went about determining the characteristics of self-actualization have been brought into question. Maslow used biographical analysis, a qualitative method whereby he searched through biographies and writings of twenty-one people that he determined were self-actualized, and then from this specific group created his list of qualities.

This means that Maslow's definition of self-actualization is based completely on his subjective vision of self-actualization, and that the definition he provides does not have to be accepted as a scientifically proven fact.

Another criticism that has been raised concerning the hierarchy of needs is Maslow's stance that the lower needs must be satisfied before someone has the ability to reach self-actualization. People who live in poverty, for example, are still capable of love or belonging, even though—according to Maslow—this should not be the case. Despite criticisms, there is no denying how important and significant Abraham Maslow was to modern psychology. He shifted attention away from abnormal behavior and made psychology focus on the positive aspects of human nature, mental health, and human potential.

THEORIES OF INTELLIGENCE
Thinking about thinking

The subject of intelligence remains one of the most controversial subjects in psychology because a standard definition of what intelligence actually is has never been agreed upon. While some believe it to be a single ability, others believe intelligence is a variety of talents, skills, and abilities. For the most part, however, it is agreed that intelligence includes a person's ability to think rationally, problem-solve, understand social norms, customs, and values, analyze situations, learn from experience, cope with life's demands, and think with reason.

Even now, psychologists disagree on whether or not intelligence can be accurately measured. When looking at intelligence, psychologists attempt to answer the following questions:

- Is intelligence inherited?

- Does the environment affect intelligence?
- Does intelligence involve a variety of skills and abilities or is it just one ability?
- Are IQ tests biased?
- Do the scores from these tests predict anything?

There are many theories that attempt to explain intelligence. Some of the major ones include:

General Intelligence

British psychologist Charles Spearman introduced the concept of general intelligence, or "g factor," in 1904. Spearman believed a general intelligence existed that influenced mental ability, and that this "g factor" could be measured with a single number from a mental ability test. He found that people who did well on one cognitive test also did well on other mental ability tests, and people who did poorly on one, also did poorly on others. Thus, he concluded, intelligence is a general cognitive ability that can be measured and expressed as a number.

Primary Mental Abilities

Psychologist Louis L. Thurstone believed there were seven "primary mental abilities" that determined intelligence. These abilities included: reasoning, verbal comprehension, numerical ability, perceptual speed, word fluency, spatial visualization, and associative memory.

Multiple Intelligences

Psychologist Howard Gardner's theory of multiple intelligences states that a numerical expression is not an accurate depiction of human intelligence. In his theory, Gardner suggests that there are actually eight distinct intelligences that are based on ability and skill, and people may be stronger in some of these intelligences and weaker in others. These are: visual-spatial intelligence (the ability to visualize things), linguistic-verbal intelligence (the ability to use words in both writing and speaking), logical-mathematical intelligence (the ability to logically analyze a problem, recognize patterns, and use reason), bodily-kinesthetic intelligence (the ability of physical control and body movement), musical intelligence (the ability to think in rhythm, sounds, and patterns), interpersonal intelligence (the ability to understand and react with others), intrapersonal intelligence (being aware of your own feelings, emotions, and motivations), and naturalistic intelligence (the ability to be in tune with nature, explore your environment, and learn more about other species).

Triarchic Theory of Intelligence

Psychologist Robert Sternberg's triarchic theory of intelligence states there are three different factors that make up "successful intelligence." They are: analytical intelligence (abilities that refer to problem-solving), creative intelligence (the ability to deal with new situations by using current skills and experiences from the past), and practical intelligence (the ability to adjust to an environment that is changing).

A TIMELINE OF INTELLIGENCE TESTING

There are as many different methods of testing intelligence as there are interpretations of what intelligence actually is. Over time, intelligence tests (known as instruments) have evolved and have become standardized.

Alfred Binet (1905)

In 1905, French psychologist Alfred Binet was hired by the French government to develop a test that would assess children's intelligence. The French government had just passed laws that required all children from the ages of six to fourteen to attend school, and so a test was warranted to see which children would need special assistance.

Binet and colleague Theodore Simon created a series of questions that concentrated on things outside of school, including memory, attention, and the ability to problem-solve.

Binet came to the realization that some children could answer questions that were more advanced and were meant for older children, while other children that were the same age could only answer questions meant for younger children.

From these findings, Binet created the concept of a mental age: the measure of intelligence that is the average abilities from children of a certain age. The Binet-Simon Scale became the first intelligence test and is the basis of what is used today.

The Stanford-Binet Intelligence Test (1916)

When the Binet-Simon Scale was brought to the United States, Stanford University psychologist Lewis Terman standardized it and used it on an American sample. The adapted version, known as the Stanford-Binet Intelligence Scale, was published in 1916.

In this test, a single number—the intelligence quotient, or IQ—was used to represent a person's score. The IQ is calculated by taking the mental age of the person, dividing it by the chronological age of the person, and then multiplying the results by 100.

Army Alpha and Army Beta Tests (1917)

During the beginning of World War I, there was an extremely large number of army recruits. To deal with screening such a large number of people, psychologist Robert Yerkes (president of the APA and chair of the Committee on the Psychological Examination of Recruits) created two intelligence tests: the Army Alpha and Army Beta tests. Over 2 million men were given the exams in an effort to determine what roles and positions they could take on.

The Wechsler Intelligence Scales (1955)

In 1955, American psychologist David Wechsler created a new intelligence test, the Wechsler Adult Intelligence Scale (WAIS). This has since been modified and is known as the WAIS-III.

He also created two tests for children: the Wechsler Preschool and Primary Scale of Intelligence (WPPSI) and the Wechsler Intelligence Scale for Children (WISC).

While the Stanford-Binet test is scored based on mental and chronological age, the Wechsler Adult Intelligence Scale is scored by looking at the individual's score and comparing it to the scores of people in the same age group. The average score is 100. The scoring method featured in the WAIS is now the standard method in IQ testing.

What Your IQ Score Means

The Stanford-Binet Intelligence Test

- 19 and below: Profound mental deficiency
- 20–49: Severe mental deficiency
- 50–69: Moderate mental deficiency
- 70–79: Mild mental deficiency
- 80–89: Dull normal
- 90–109: Average or normal
- 110–119: Superior
- 120–139: Very superior
- 140 and higher: Genius or near-genius

The Wechsler Intelligence Scale for Children

- 69 and below: Extremely low intelligence
- 70–79: Borderline low
- 80–89: Low average
- 90–109: Average
- 110–119: High average
- 120–129: Superior
- 130 and higher: Extremely superior

KURT LEWIN (1890–1947)

The father of modern social psychology

Kurt Lewin was born on September 9th, 1890, in Mogilno, Prussia (modern-day Poland), to a middle-class Jewish family. In 1909, Lewin attended the University of Freiberg to study medicine; however, he then transferred to the University of Munich, where he decided to pursue biology.

In 1910, Lewin began attending the University of Berlin to earn a doctorate degree in philosophy and psychology; and in 1914, he earned his degree in psychology. Following this, Lewin entered World War I, working in the infantry division. He fought in the war for four years, until he was wounded in action.

In 1917, Lewin married a schoolteacher by the name of Maria Landsberg. Their marriage only lasted ten years, but the two would have two children together. Then, in 1929, Lewin married Gertrud

Weiss, with whom he would have two more children.

Kurt Lewin began lecturing at the Psychological Institute of the University of Berlin in the subjects of psychology and philosophy in 1921. He was extremely popular with students and was already a prolific writer. In 1930, he was invited by Stanford University to be a visiting professor. Lewin eventually immigrated to the United States, becoming a naturalized citizen in 1940.

When the United States entered World War II, Lewin used his research to aid in the war effort and acted as a consultant for the United States government. In 1944, Lewin created the Commission on Community Interrelations (CCI), which focused on fighting religious and racial discrimination, and he created the Research Center for Group Dynamics at M.I.T., which focused on the study of groups and how groups affect the behavior of an individual.

Kurt Lewin is considered to be the father of modern social psychology. He was one of the first psychologists to use scientific methods and experimentation to examine social behaviors. In his lifetime, Lewin published eight books and over eighty articles.

On February 12th, 1947, Kurt Lewin suffered a heart attack and died. He was fifty-seven years old.

LEWIN'S FIELD THEORY

Lewin was inspired by Gestalt psychology and was also greatly influenced by Albert Einstein's field theory, which stated that objects are continuously interacting with gravity and electromagnetism. Lewin attempted to apply this Einsteinian idea to psychology, and postulated that behavior was the result of the individual continuously interacting with their environment.

Lewin believed that behavior was determined by the entirety of a person's situation, and came to refer to the sum of these coexisting factors as a "field." According to Lewin's theory, a person will behave differently depending on how tensions that are perceived between the self and the environment are worked out. In order to fully understand behavior, the entire psychological field, whether school, work, church, family—what Lewin referred to as a "lifespace"—had to be looked at.

Lewin's field theory had a huge influence in social psychology and helped popularize the idea that behavior is caused by the interaction of the environment and the individual's traits.

LEADERSHIP STYLES

In 1939, Kurt Lewin led a group of researchers to target and study different types of leadership styles. While the number of leadership styles has since been expanded upon, Lewin and his group originally identified three types: authoritarian, democratic, and laissez-fair. For the study, schoolchildren were placed into three groups with a leader that corresponded with one of the three styles of leadership. Lewin and his group of researchers then studied the responses of children as the leader directed the kids in an arts and crafts project.

Authoritarian or Autocratic Leadership

Authoritarian leaders give clear explanations of what has to be done, when something should be done by, and how something should be done. These types of leaders make decisions with little to no input from the other people in the group; and because of this, there is an obvious division between the leader and those who follow the leader.

Under an authoritarian leader, Lewin found that there was less creativity in decision-making. If a leader abuses their power in authoritarian leadership, they are often seen as bossy, dictatorial, and controlling. An authoritarian leader is best for situations where the leader is the most knowledgeable individual in the group or when there is very little time for decisions to be made as a group. Lewin also observed that it is more difficult to move to a democratic leadership from an authoritarian leadership than from a democratic leadership to an authoritarian leadership.

Democratic or Participative Leadership

Lewin's results showed that a democratic leadership was the most effective style. Democratic leaders participate in the group, allow input from others, and offer guidance. Lewin found that the children participating in this group were less productive than the children in the authoritative group, but that their contributions were higher in quality. While democratic leaders have the final say over decision-making, other group members are encouraged to participate, and this makes them feel more engaged and motivated in the process, which results in them being more creative.

Laissez-Fair or Delegative Leadership

In a laissez-fair leadership, the leader takes a hands-off approach and leaves all decision-making up to the group. Lewin found that this type of leadership style was the least productive. He noted that children placed in this group demanded more from the leader, could not work independently, and showed very little cooperation. If members of a group are highly qualified in particular areas, a laissez-fair type of leadership can be effective; however, most of the time it leads to a lack of motivation from group members and poorly defined roles.

Kurt Lewin's focus on behavior of the individual in relation to their environment—and not past experiences—was groundbreaking work, and Lewin is considered by many to be one of the founding fathers of social psychology. His incorporation of Gestalt principles, understanding of situational influences, and work in group dynamics and leadership greatly impacted how psychologists approach and understand social behavior.

CARL JUNG (1875–1961)

Introverts, extroverts, and the unconscious

Carl Jung was born on July 26th, 1875, in Kesswil, Switzerland. The son of a pastor, Jung was the only child out of four to survive. Jung's mother battled with depression and was frequently absent from his home until the family moved to Basel when Jung was four years old.

Jung recalled that as a child, he preferred to be in isolation, and felt happiest when he was alone. In 1887, at the age of twelve, Jung was thrown to the ground by a classmate and became unconscious. As a result of this incident, Jung began to suffer from neurotic fainting spells. Though he quickly noticed that fainting allowed him to get out of going to school, these fainting episodes were not fake, but were actually the result of neuroses. For six months, Jung stayed home and doctors feared he suffered from epilepsy. One day, Jung overheard his father talking to someone about how he feared that Carl would never be able to support himself. From that day on, Jung decided to turn his attention towards academics. Prior to returning to his studies, Jung still suffered from fainting; but eventually, he was able to overcome his problem and go back to school. He never experienced this fainting problem again. Later in life, he recalled that this was the first time that he encountered neurosis.

In 1895, Carl Jung attended the University of Basel to study medicine. One day, Jung discovered a book about spiritualistic phenomena. Jung became so intrigued with the subject and psychiatry that in the last months of his studies, he switched his attention from medicine to psychiatry. To him, psychiatry was the perfect combination of medicine and spirituality. In 1902, Jung finished his doctoral dissertation, "On the Psychology and Pathology of So-Called Occult Phenomena," and graduated with a medical degree.

In 1903, Jung married Emma Rauschenbach and began working at the

Burgholzli Psychiatric Hospital. Though he and his wife would remain married until she died in 1955, Jung did have affairs with other women, including a years-long relationship with his first patient from the Burgholzli Psychiatric Hospital.

In 1906, Jung began his correspondence with Sigmund Freud. He sent Freud a collection of his work, entitled *Studies in Word Association*, and the two men soon became good friends. Jung's friendship with Freud would have a profound impact on his work, especially on his interest in the unconscious mind. However, beginning in 1909, Jung began disagreeing with some of Freud's ideas. While Freud placed an emphasis on sex as the motivation behind behavior, Jung became more interested in symbols, dreams, and self-analysis. By 1912, Jung and Freud's friendship broke apart.

Because Jung renounced Freud's sex theory, the psychoanalytic community turned against Carl Jung, and he was cut off from several associates and friends. It is during this time that Jung devoted his time to exploring his subconscious and created analytic psychology.

Jung believed every person's purpose in life was to have his or her conscious and unconscious become fully integrated, so that they could become their "true self." He called this "individuation."

Carl Jung also took an interest in what he referred to as "primitive psychology," and studied different cultures found in India, East Africa, and the Pueblo Indians in New Mexico. On June 6th, 1961, Carl Jung died in Zurich.

Doctoral Definitions

Individuation: By listening to the messages found within our waking imagination and dreams, a person can understand, express, and harmonize the many parts of their unique psyche to reach their "true self." According to Jung, within everyone's unconscious are primordial images, which he called "archetypes," that are reflections of universal themes and patterns. These primordial images are unlearned and act in a similar fashion to instincts, and help organize our experiences.

ARCHETYPES

Like Freud, Carl Jung believed the human psyche was made up of three parts, though his conception was somewhat different than Freud's. Jung believed that the psyche could be divided into the ego, the collective unconscious, and the personal unconscious. Jung claimed the ego was a representation of the conscious mind, the collective unconscious contained experiences and information that we all share as a species—which he believed was a form of psychological inheritance—and the personal unconscious contained memories, both available and suppressed.

Jung claimed that archetypes, or primordial images that reflect common patterns, exist in the collective unconscious and help organize how a person experiences particular things. These are not learned, but rather are hereditary, universal, and innate. Archetypes can combine and overlap, and while there is no limit to how many archetypes there may be, Jung recognized four of primary importance:

1. **The Self:** This archetype represents the union of the conscious and the unconscious, and this archetype is symbolic of a strive for unity and wholeness. This occurs through individuation, when every part of an individual's personality is expressed equally and the individual has a more balanced psyche. The self is often represented in dreams as a circle, mandala, or square.
2. **The Shadow:** This archetype is comprised of instincts regarding life and sex, and is made up of weaknesses, desires, shortcomings, and repressed ideas. The shadow archetype is part of the unconscious mind, and can represent the unknown, chaos, and wildness. The shadow can

appear in dreams as a snake, a dragon, a demon, or any other dark, exotic, or wild figure.

3. **The Anima or Animus:** In the male psyche, the anima is a feminine image, and in the female psyche, the animus is a male image. When the anima and the animus are combined, it is called a "syzygy." Syzygy creates wholeness, and one obvious example of a syzygy is when two people have determined they are soul mates, thus combining the anima and the animus. Syzygy is also known as the divine couple, and represents wholeness, unification, and a feeling of completeness. For this reason, the anima and animus are representative of a person's "true self," and are a main source of communication with the collective unconscious.
4. **The Persona:** This is how a person presents him or herself to the world. The persona protects

the ego from negative images, and can appear in dreams in many different forms. The persona is a representation of the many masks a person wears in situations and among different groups of people.

Other archetypes Jung recognized include the father (representative of authority and power), the mother (representative of comfort and nurturing), the child (representative of a desire for innocence and salvation), and the wise old man (representative of wisdom, guidance, and knowledge).

Carl Jung's Relation to Alcoholics Anonymous

In the early 1930s, a man known as Rowland H. met with Jung for help with his severe alcoholism. After several sessions of showing no improvement, Jung believed Rowland's condition to be hopeless and declared that the only way for the man to find relief was through a spiritual experience. Jung suggested an evangelical Christian group known as the Oxford Group. Rowland took Jung's advice and introduced another alcoholic, known as Ebby T., to the group. Ebby would become extremely successful with the Oxford Group and invite an old drinking buddy, known only as Bill W., to join the group. Eventually, Bill W. would have his own spiritual awakening, and he would go on to become one of the founders of Alcoholics Anonymous. In 1961, Bill W. wrote a letter to Carl Jung, thanking him.

Carl Jung is considered the founder of analytical psychology, which approached psychoanalysis by understanding the unconscious and an individual's desire to become whole. Jung's ideas on extraversion, introversion, dreams, and symbols were extremely influential to psychotherapy and understanding personality psychology.

HENRY MURRAY (1893–1988)

Personality traits

Henry Murray was born on May 13th, 1893, in New York, New York, to a wealthy family. In 1915, Murray graduated from Harvard University with a degree in history. He then attended Columbia University's College of Physicians and Surgeons where he received an MD in biology. It was at Columbia that Murray first began taking an interest in psychology.

Murray was fascinated with the work of Carl Jung; and in 1925, Murray met with Jung in Zurich. Murray recalled that the two men talked for hours, went sailing, and smoked, and that this meeting actually led him to experience his unconscious. It was from his meeting with Jung that Murray decided to formally pursue a career in psychology.

Henry Murray soon became an instructor at the Harvard Psychological

Clinic at the request of Morton Prince, its founder. By 1937, Murray was named director of the clinic. With his extensive medical background and analytical training, Murray brought a unique twist to the work he was doing, which focused on personality and the unconscious.

In 1938, Henry Murray left Harvard to help with the war effort, and was even asked to create a psychological profile of Adolf Hitler. That same year, Murray created the now-famous Thematic Apperception Test (TAT), a test that set out to determine unconscious motivation and personality themes. During World War II, Murray created and directed the Office of Strategic Services, which assessed the psychological fitness of agents within the American intelligence agencies.

Murray returned to Harvard University in 1947, and in 1949, he helped create the Psychological Clinic Annex. Murray became an emeritus professor at Harvard University in 1962. On June 23rd, 1988, Henry Murray died of pneumonia. He was ninety-five years old.

MURRAY'S THEORY OF PSYCHOGENIC NEEDS

In 1938, Henry Murray came up with his theory of psychogenic needs. This theory describes personality as being the result of basic needs that are found mostly at the unconscious level. The two most basic types of needs are:

1. **Primary needs:** Biological needs like food, water, and oxygen.
2. **Secondary needs:** Psychological needs including the need to achieve, be nurtured, or be independent.

Furthermore, Murray and his colleagues identified twenty-seven needs that he claimed all people had (though each person has different levels of each need). The needs are:

- **Abasement:** The need to accept punishment and surrender

- **Achievement:** The need to succeed and be able to overcome obstacles
- **Acquisition or Conservance:** The need to attain possessions
- **Affiliation:** The need to make friendships and relations
- **Aggression:** The need to harm others
- **Autonomy:** The need to remain strong and resist others
- **Blame avoidance:** The need to obey rules and avoid blame
- **Construction:** The need to create and build
- **Contrariance:** The need to be unique
- **Counteraction:** The need to defend one's honor
- **Defendance:** The need to justify one's actions
- **Deference:** The need to serve or follow someone who is one's superior
- **Dominance or Power:** The need to lead other people and control

- **Exhibition:** The need to draw attention
- **Exposition:** The need to educate and give information
- **Harm avoidance:** The need to avoid pain
- **Infavoidance:** The need to hide weaknesses and avoid shame or failure
- **Nurturance:** The need to protect those that are helpless
- **Order:** The need to organize, arrange, and be particular
- **Play:** The need to have fun, relax, and relieve tension or stress
- **Recognition:** The need to gain social status and approval by displaying one's achievements
- **Rejection:** The need to reject others
- **Sentience:** The need to enjoy sensuous experiences
- **Sex or Erotic:** The need to create and enjoy an erotic relationship
- **Similance:** The need to empathize with others

- **Succorance:** The need to obtain sympathy or protection
- **Understanding or Cognizance:** The need to ask questions, seek knowledge, analyze, and experience

Murray believed that each individual need was important, but that needs could also be interrelated, could support other needs, or could be in conflict with various other needs. According to Murray, the way these needs are displayed in our behavior is, in part, due to environmental factors, which Murray referred to as "presses."

THEMATIC APPERCEPTION TEST

Murray's Thematic Apperception Test attempts to tap into the patient's unconscious, evaluate patterns of thought, and reveal personality and emotional responses by showing a person various ambiguous, but provocative, pictures and having them tell a story about what they see in the picture. The basic outline of the test is as follows:

1. Have the participant look at the following picture for a few moments.
2. Based on the picture, instruct the participant to narrate a story and include:

- What led to the event you see in this picture?
- What is happening at this exact moment?
- What are the characters in the picture thinking and feeling?
- What is the outcome of this story?

The actual test involves thirty-one pictures that feature men, women, children, figures of ambiguous gender, nonhuman figures, and one completely blank image.

The stories are recorded and then analyzed for underlying attitudes, needs, and patterns of reaction. Two commonly used formal scoring methods include the

Defense Mechanisms Manual (otherwise known as DMM), which assesses denial, projection, and identification; and the Social Cognition and Object Relations Scale (otherwise known as SCORS), which analyzes different dimensions of the psyche in its environment.

MURRAY'S ANALYSIS OF ADOLF HITLER

In 1943, Murray was commissioned by the Allied Forces to help them understand the psychological makeup of Adolf Hitler. Murray concluded that Hitler's personality type was one that held grudges, had the tendency to belittle, blame, and bully, did not have a high tolerance of criticism, could not take a joke, could not express gratitude, sought revenge, and was in high demand for attention. Murray also stated Hitler lacked qualities of a balanced personality and that he had an extremely strong self-trust and self-will. Lastly, Murray correctly guessed that should Germany lose the war, Hitler would kill himself in a very dramatic way;

and as a result, Murray feared that Hitler would become a martyr in the process.

Henry Murray's work in psychogenic needs and understanding of personality was extremely important because he not only emphasized the unconscious, but also biological factors. His Thematic Apperception Test is still used to this day.

LEFT AND RIGHT BRAIN

Thinking from your side

The left and right sides of the brain have specific functions and are responsible for different types of thinking. Most interestingly, these two sides of the brain have the ability to operate practically independently of each other. In psychology, this is referred to as the lateralization of brain function.

In the early 1960s, psychobiologist Roger Sperry began conducting experiments on epileptic patients. Sperry discovered that by cutting the structure responsible for connecting and communicating between the left and right hemispheres of the brain, known as the corpus callosum, seizures could be reduced and even eliminated.

Once the corpus callosum was cut, the patients—who originally appeared normal—began experiencing other strange symptoms. Many patients found that they could name objects that had been processed by the left hemisphere of the brain, but could no longer name objects that were processed by the right hemisphere. From this, Sperry deduced that the left hemisphere of the brain was responsible for controlling language. Other patients struggled with the ability to put blocks together in a prearranged way.

Sperry was able to successfully show that the left and right hemispheres of the brain were responsible for different functions, and that each hemisphere also had the ability to learn. In 1981, Roger Sperry was awarded the Nobel Prize for his work in brain lateralization.

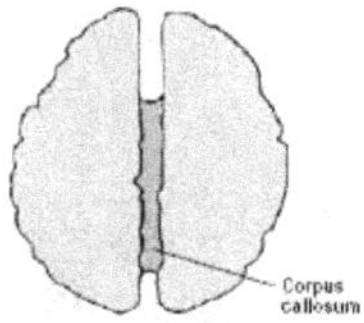

LEFT BRAIN AND RIGHT BRAIN DIVISION

RIGHT BRAIN DOMINANCE

The right hemisphere of the brain, which is responsible for the left side of the body, is more capable in tasks that are expressive and creative—also known as visual construction tasks. These include tasks such as expressing and reading emotions, understanding metaphors, discriminating shapes (like picking out an object that is camouflaged), copying designs, and making music.

LEFT BRAIN DOMINANCE

The left hemisphere of the brain, which is responsible for the right side of the body, is more capable at tasks such as language, critical thinking, logic, reasoning, and the use of numbers.

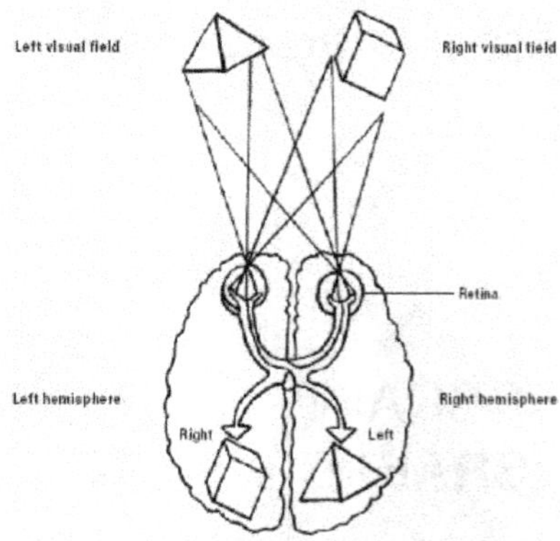

DETAILED EXAMPLE OF LEFT AND RIGHT BRAIN SPLIT

THE SPLIT-BRAIN EXPERIMENTS

In Roger Sperry's split-brain experiments, Sperry had a split-brain patient (someone with a cut corpus callosum) sit in front of a screen that would hide his or her hands. Behind this screen, Sperry placed objects that the split-brain patient could not see.

The patient would then focus their eyes to the center of the screen and a word would appear on the screen in the patient's left visual field. This information was then received by the right hemisphere of the brain (the nonverbal part). The result was that the patient was actually unable to tell Sperry the word that he or she had seen.

Sperry would then ask the patient to use their left hand to reach behind the screen and choose the object that corresponded with the word. Even though the patient was not aware of even seeing a word, the patient was able to choose the correct object. This is because the right hemisphere controls the movement of the left side of the body.

Through this experiment, Roger Sperry was able to successfully show that the left hemisphere of the brain is responsible for controlling reading and speech, and that the right hemisphere of the brain does not have the ability to process verbal stimuli.

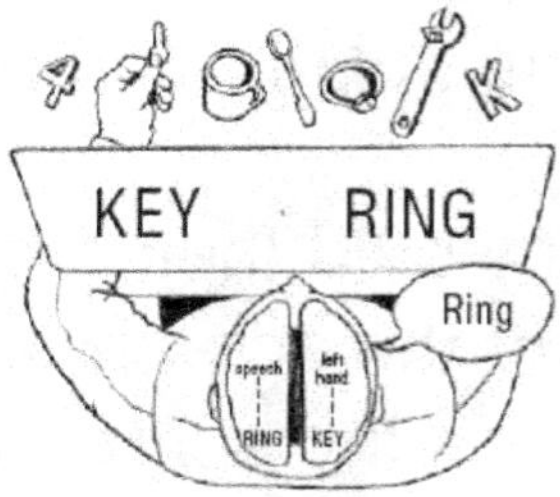

VISUALIZATION OF THE SPLIT BRAIN EXPERIMENT

So I Know My Dominant Side ... Now What?

Understanding which hemisphere you are more dominant in can actually be incredibly useful when it comes to thinking of better ways to approach studying or learning. For example, if you are more dominant with your right hemisphere, you may have a harder time following verbal instructions, and might benefit from improving your organizational skills or writing directions down.

LOVE

Listening to your heart

Love may be one of the most complex human emotions, but also possibly the most central too. There are many different theories regarding love, and while psychologists agree that love is a central human emotion, they are still unsure exactly why it happens, or how. At present, there are four primary theories that attempt to explain love, emotional attachment, and liking.

RUBIN'S SCALES OF LIKING AND LOVING

Psychologist Zick Rubin was one of the first people to create a method of empirically measuring love. Rubin believed that romantic love was composed of three elements: attachment, caring, and intimacy.

- **Attachment:** The need to be with another person and be cared for. Important components of attachment include approval and physical contact.
- **Caring:** Valuing the happiness and needs of the other person just as much as you value your own.
- **Intimacy:** Communicating your private desires, feelings, and beliefs.

Rubin then created two questionnaires that would be able to measure these elements. According to Rubin, the difference between liking someone and loving someone can be seen in how we evaluate the other person. Rubin's questions were then created to measure feelings of liking another person and feelings of loving another person, and then these results were compared. When Rubin gave the questionnaire to a group of participants, he told them to base their answers on how they felt about a good friend and how they felt about their significant other. He found that, while the scores about the good friends were high on the liking scale, only the scores regarding significant others rated high on the loving scale. Thus, Rubin was able to successfully measure feelings of love.

ELAINE HATFIELD'S PASSIONATE AND COMPASSIONATE LOVE

Psychologist Elaine Hatfield claimed that there were only two forms of love: passionate and compassionate love.

- **Passionate love:** Feelings of intense sexual arousal, attraction, affection, emotion, and a strong urge to be with one another. Passionate love tends to be short-lived, lasting from six to thirty months, but can lead to compassionate love.
- **Compassionate love:** Feelings of attachment, respect, trust, affection, and commitment. Compassionate love lasts longer than passionate love.

Hatfield also differentiated between reciprocated love, which leads to feelings of elation and fulfillment, and unreciprocated love, which leads to feelings of desperation and despair. She believed there were certain key factors that had to exist for compassionate and passionate love to occur. These include:

- **Timing:** When an individual is ready to fall and be in love.
- **Similarity:** A person has the tendency to fall passionately in love with an individual that is similar to him or herself.
- **Early attachment styles:** Long-term and deeper relationships are often the result of people who are strongly attached to one another, while people who fall in and out of love often generally do not have a strong attachment or connection.

JOHN LEE'S SIX STYLES OF LOVE

John Lee believed the different styles of love were similar to the rules of a color wheel. Much like the way a color wheel features three primary colors, Lee believed that love could be broken down into three basic primary styles. These are:

- **Eros:** Loving the ideal of a person both physically and emotionally.
- **Ludos:** A type of love that is played like a game or conquest (and might result in many partners at one time).
- **Storge:** Love that stems from a friendship over time.

Just like the primary colors of a color wheel can be combined and create complimentary colors, so too can the primary love styles. The result is three secondary styles of love:

- **Mania:** A combination of Eros and Ludos, Mania is a style of love that is obsessive. This includes emotional highs and lows, jealousy, and very possessive feelings.

- **Pragma:** A combination of Ludos and Storge, Pragma is a love that is practical. Lovers go into the situation with the hopes of reaching their final goal. Expectations of the relationship are thought about practically and realistically.
- **Agape:** A combination of Eros and Storge, Agape is a love that is all-encompassing and selfless.

ROBERT STERNBERG'S TRIANGULAR THEORY OF LOVE

In this 2004 theory, Robert Sternberg proposed that love could be broken down into three parts: intimacy, passion, and commitment.

- **Intimacy:** Closeness, supporting one another, sharing with one another, and feeling loved.
- **Passion:** Feelings of sexual arousal and attraction, and

euphoria. This is what drives two individuals together.

- **Commitment:** The desire to remain loyal to another person and stay in a long-term relationship.

From these three components, seven different combinations can be created. The easiest way to understand this is by looking at it as a triangle. In the triangle, intimacy, passion, and commitment are the vertices, and the seven combinations are the connections between these vertices.

Alternatively, here is another way to look at it:

	INTIMACY	PASSION	COMMITMENT
Nonlove			
Friendship/Liking	X		
Infatuation/Limerance		X	
Empty Love			X
Romantic Love	X	X	
Companionate Love	X		X
Fatuous Love		X	X
Consummate Love	X	X	X

VISUALIZATION OF STERNBERG'S THEORY OF LOVE

- **Liking or Friendship:** This represents a friendship where there is closeness and a strong bond, but there is not any passion or commitment present.
- **Infatuation or Limerance:** This is what a person feels when he or she experiences "love at first sight." Because there is no commitment or intimacy, infatuation can be fleeting.
- **Empty Love:** This is when a love has lost intimacy and passion, but there is still a strong commitment between the two people.

- **Romantic Love:** Romantic love features intimacy and passion, meaning there is sexual arousal and an emotional bond, but there is a lack of commitment.
- **Companionate Love:** This is a type of love where passion does not exist or no longer exists, but there is still a great commitment and deep affection for one another. This type of love is found among family members, close friends, and can even be found in marriages.
- **Fatuous Love:** This is a type of love that only features passion and commitment, but lacks intimacy. An example of fatuous love is a brief or impulsive marriage.
- **Consummate Love:** This is the ideal form of love, and it features intimacy, passion, and commitment. Sternberg claimed that once consummate love was achieved, it would be even harder to maintain and that it may not be permanent. If, for example, passion becomes lost with the passage of time, then

the consummate love would turn into companionate love.

During the lifespan of a relationship, Sternberg believed that the balance between intimacy, passion, and commitment would shift. Understanding the three components of love and the seven types can help couples recognize what they need to improve upon, what they should avoid, and even when it might be time to end the relationship.

KAREN HORNEY (1885–1952)

Women, neuroses, and breaking away from Freud

Karen Horney (née Karen Danielsen) was born on September 16th, 1885, in the fishing village of Blankenese, Germany. Horney's father, a ship captain, was a strict and very religious man who often ignored Horney and seemed to like her brother, Berndt, more than her.

At the age of nine, Karen developed a crush on her older brother, Berndt. When he rejected her feelings, Karen fell into a depression, which she would battle throughout her life. Karen saw herself as an unattractive girl and believed that doing well in school would be the best option for her to succeed in life.

In 1906, at the age of twenty-one, Karen attended medical school at the University of Freiburg Medical School. Three years later, Karen would marry a law student by the name of Oscar

Horney; and from 1910 to 1916, they would have three children together. Horney transferred first to the University of Gottingen, before finally graduating from the University of Berlin in 1913. Within a single year, Horney's parents died and she had her first child. To cope with her emotions, she began seeing Karl Abraham, a psychoanalyst who was a disciple of Freud. Abraham would eventually become Horney's mentor at the Berlin Psychoanalytic Society.

In 1920, Horney began working as a lecturer for the Berlin Psychoanalytic Society. In 1923, Horney's brother died. Her brother's death was extremely difficult for Horney and she fell into another bout of depression. In 1926, Horney separated from her husband; and in 1930, she and her three daughters moved to the United States, where they ended up residing in a Jewish German part of Brooklyn, New York. It was while living here that Horney became friends with famous psychologists like Erich Fromm and Harry Stack Sullivan.

Horney soon became the Associate Director of the Chicago Institute for

Psychoanalysis, where she first began working on her most influential work: her theories on neuroses and personality. Two years later, Horney returned to New York and worked at both the New York Psychoanalytic Institute and the New School for Social Research. Though Horney had begun disputing the work of Sigmund Freud while still living in Germany, when she came to the States, her opposition towards Freud's work grew so much that, in 1941, she was forced to resign from the New York Psychoanalytic Institute. Horney then went on to establish the American Institute for Psychoanalysis that same year. Horney published her books, *The Neurotic Personality of Our Time* in 1937, and *Self-Analysis* in 1942.

Karen Horney is perhaps most known for her work on the subject of neuroses, for disagreeing and breaking away from Sigmund Freud's views on women, and for sparking an interest in the psychology of women. Horney was also a firm believer that the individual had the ability to be his or her own therapist, and emphasized the significance of self-help and self-analysis. Karen Horney died of cancer on December 4th, 1952. She was sixty-seven years old.

THE PSYCHOLOGY OF WOMEN

Karen Horney never studied under Sigmund Freud, but she was incredibly familiar with his work and even taught psychoanalysis at the Berlin Psychoanalytic Institute and the New York Psychoanalytic Institute, where her views on his work eventually led to her departure from the school.

You may recall in Sigmund Freud's stages of psychosexual development that at the phallic stage—ages three to six—Freud claimed that the relationship between young girls and their fathers was the result of penis envy.

Horney disagreed with Freud's notion of penis envy and viewed it as demeaning and incorrect. Rather, she claimed that at this stage, something she referred to as "womb envy" occurs—the man's envy that a woman can bear children. As a result, the male tries to compensate for his feelings of inferiority by attempting to succeed in other ways. In other words, because the male cannot reproduce, he tries to leave his mark on the world in some alternative aspect.

Horney also argued that Freud was wrong in his belief that males and females had fundamental differences in their personalities. While Freud took a biological approach, Horney claimed that without the cultural and societal restrictions that are often placed on women, men and women would be equal. This idea was not accepted at the time; however, it later resonated, after Horney's death, in helping promote gender equality.

KAREN HORNEY'S THEORY OF NEUROSES

Karen Horney's theory of neuroses is one of the best-known theories on the topic. She believed that interpersonal relationships created basic anxiety, and that neuroses developed as a method to deal with these relationships. Horney identified three categories that neurotic needs could be classified under. If an individual is well-adjusted, he or she will be able to apply all three strategies. A person only becomes neurotic when one or more of these are overused. The categories are:

Needs that move an individual towards other people

These are neurotic needs that will make an individual seek out the acceptance, help, or affirmation from others in order to feel worthy. These type of people need to be appreciated and liked by those around them, and may come off as clingy or needy.

Needs that move an individual against other people

In an effort to feel good about themselves, people will deal with their anxiety by trying to force their power onto other people and control those around them. People that express these needs are seen as unkind, selfish, bossy, and controlling. Horney stated that people would project their hostilities onto others in a process she referred to as externalization. The individual would then be able to use this as a justification for his or her sometimes cruel behavior.

Needs that move an individual away from other people

These neurotic needs are responsible for antisocial behavior, and a person may appear indifferent to other people. The mentality behind this approach is if an individual does not get involved with other people, then other people cannot then hurt the individual. This can lead to feelings of emptiness and loneliness.

Horney then identified ten neurotic needs within these categories:

- **Moving Towards Other People**
    1. **The need for affection and approval:** This is the desire to meet other people's expectations, make others happy, and be liked. Those that experience this need are afraid of hostility or anger from other people, and are very sensitive to any rejection or criticism.

2. **An individual's need for a partner that will control his or her life:** This need involves a strong fear of being abandoned, and the belief that having a partner in one's life can resolve any trouble or problems that he or she may be having.

- **Moving Against Other People**

1. **The need to have power:** Individuals with this need control and dominate others because they hate weakness but admire, and are desperate for, strength.
2. **The need to exploit other people:** Individuals with this need are manipulative and believe people exist to be used. Associations with other people are only used to attain things such as control, sex, or money.
3. **The need for prestige:** These are individuals that need acclaim and public recognition. Social status, material possessions, professional accomplishments, personality traits,

and even loved ones are judged based on prestige, and there is a fear of public embarrassment.

4. **The need for personal achievement:** Pushing oneself to achieve is perfectly normal. However, neurotic individuals may become desperate to achieve, and push themselves as a result of their own insecurities. There is a fear of failure, and the need to always accomplish more than others.
5. **The need for personal admiration:** These are individuals that are narcissistic and wish to be viewed based off of an ideal version of themselves, instead of who they actually are.

- **Moving Away from Other People**

1. **The need for perfection:** An individual with this need will commonly be in fear of personal flaws, and will search for these flaws so that he or she can quickly conceal or change them.

2. **The need for independence:** In an effort to not depend on, or be tied down to, other people, an individual exhibiting this need might distance him or herself from others. This creates a "loner" mentality.
3. **The need to limit one's life so that it remains within narrow borders:** The preference for individuals with this need is to go unnoticed and remain inconspicuous. These individuals will often undervalue their own skills and talents, will not demand much, will not desire material objects, are content with very little, and regard their own needs as secondary.

Karen Horney was incredibly influential to the world of psychology. Her views on neuroses as a way to deal with interpersonal relationships and her identification of neurotic needs were truly groundbreaking, and by breaking away from the male-dominant views set forth by Sigmund Freud, Horney established herself as a strong voice for women and female psychology.

JOHN BOWLBY (1907 -1990)

The father of the theory of motherly love

John Bowlby was born in London, England, on February 26th, 1907, to an upper-middle class family. Bowlby's father, Sir Anthony Alfred Bowlby, was a Baronet and worked as a member of the King's medical staff. Bowlby only interacted with his mother for about an hour each day, as was customary for that social class during this period. At the time, it was commonly believed that showing one's child affection and care would lead to spoiling. As one of six children, Bowlby became very close with his nanny instead. At the age of four, Bowlby's nanny left, and he experienced such a deep sadness that he compared it to losing a mother.

When Bowlby was seven years old, his family sent him to a boarding school. Bowlby would later recall this event as being quite traumatic to his development. This experience, however, would prove to have a large and lasting impact on Bowlby, whose work in psychology focused on how a child's development is affected when he or she is separated from their caregiver.

Bowlby attended Trinity College, Cambridge, where he studied psychology; and following graduation, he began working with delinquent and maladjusted children. At the age of twenty-two, Bowlby began attending the University College Hospital in London, where he studied medicine. While he was a student in medical school, Bowlby enrolled in the Institute for Psychoanalysis. By 1937, Bowlby was working as a psychoanalyst at the Maudsley Hospital.

When World War II came around, Bowlby served as a member of the Royal Army Medical Corps. In 1938, Bowlby married Ursula Longstaff, with whom he would have four children. When the war ended, he became the Deputy Director of the Tavistock Clinic in London. During the 1950s, Bowlby briefly worked as a mental health consultant for the World Health Organization, where he would create some of his most influential work, like his attachment theory.

Today, John Bowlby is most well-known for his wide-ranging work in child development. In particular, drawing from examples throughout his own life history, Bowlby focused on how separation from a child's caregiver affects the development of a child and the practical applications of what that separation means for the growing youth. John Bowlby died on September 2nd, 1990. He was eighty-three years old.

BOWLBY'S ATTACHMENT THEORY

John Bowlby is considered to be the first attachment theorist, generally defined as a psychologist who considers how early attachments shape peoples' lives. According to Bowlby, attachment is the psychological bond between any two people. Bowlby believed that in order to survive, children are preprogrammed to create attachments. Furthermore, the earliest bonds that form are those between child and caregiver, and these can leave a lasting impact on the rest of an individual's life. Attachment is responsible for improving the chance of survival for a child because it is the psychological force that keeps a child close to his or her mother.

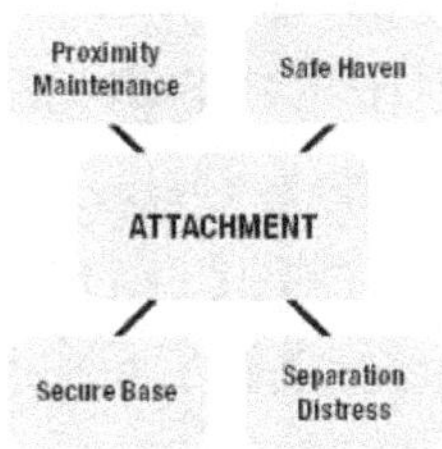

ILLUSTRATION OF PSYCHOLOGICAL BONDS

In his attachment theory, John Bowlby claimed that a child will possess the sense of security that allows for exploration only when the child's mother has been available and responsive.

In Bowlby's conception, there are four characteristics to attachment:

1. **Safe Haven:** If a child ever feels scared, threatened, or in danger,

the caregiver comforts, supports, and soothes the child.

2. **Secure Base:** The caregiver provides the child with a secure foundation so that the child can learn, explore the world, and sort things out on his or her own.
3. **Proximity Maintenance:** Even though the child can explore the world, he or she still tries to stay close to the caregiver to stay safe.
4. **Separation Distress:** The child becomes upset, unhappy, and distressed when separated from his or her caregiver.

Only one primary attachment is formed with babies, most commonly with the mother, and it occurs within the child's first year (this is known as monotropy). If this type of bond does not occur or breaks down, it can have serious consequences on the child, and even lead to affectionless psychopathy. If attachment is not present by the time the child is three years old, then the child will never have it. Furthermore:

- Attachment from the caregiver must be secure in order to create positive social, intellectual, and emotional development.
- If attachment has been formed and is then interrupted, there will be serious consequences to the child's social, intellectual, and emotional development.
- The critical period for a baby to be with his or her caregiver is between six and twenty-four months.

Doctoral Definitions

Maternal deprivation: The term Bowlby used to describe the developmental impairment caused by a child being separated from his or her mother. Long-term consequences of maternal deprivation include diminished intelligence, depression, heightened aggression, delinquency, and affectionless psychopathy (a lack of remorse, the inability to have emotional relationships, a lack of impulse control, and chronic anger).

BOWLBY'S FORTY-FOUR THIEVES STUDY

To test how important to socialization the relationship between a mother and her child is during the first five years, Bowlby conducted an experiment with forty-four adolescent juvenile delinquents. Bowlby believed that a higher rate of juvenile delinquency, antisocial conduct, and emotional difficulties could be directly linked to a disruption of this important attachment. Essentially, Bowlby set out to see if maternal deprivation could be linked to adolescent delinquency. Interviews were held with forty-four adolescent juvenile delinquents. These adolescent juvenile delinquents were all placed in a child guidance clinic because of stealing. Bowlby also used forty-four other adolescents from the clinic as a control. It should be noted that these adolescents were actually determined to be emotionally disturbed, but had never stolen. Bowlby then interviewed the parents of the adolescent juvenile delinquents and the control group, looking to see if the children had ever experienced separation from their parents in their first five years of development, and how long the separation lasted.

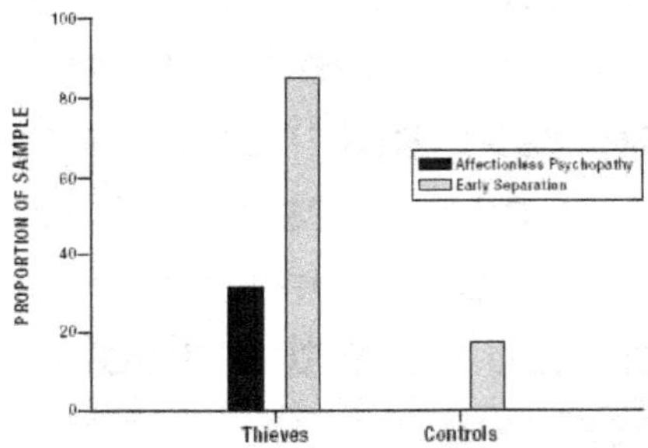

SOCIAL RELATIONSHIPS IN BOWLBY'S STUDY

Bowlby found that, during the first five years, more than half of the juvenile delinquent thieves were separated from their mothers for periods of time greater than six months; and in the control group, only two adolescents had experienced a similar separation. While Bowlby found that no adolescent in the control group showed affectionless psychopathy, he said 32 percent of the juvenile delinquent thieves did show affectionless psychopathy. From this research, Bowlby came to the conclusion that there is a correlation between adolescent criminal behavior and maternal deprivation as a child.

Of course, Bowlby's findings in this study can be disputed. Not only does the experiment rely on interviews and memories, which have the possibility of being inaccurate, but there may also be experimenter bias because Bowlby designed and conducted his experiment, and determined what the diagnosis of affectionless psychopathy was.

By drawing upon his own life experiences, John Bowlby created a completely new field of study within psychology, and the impact of his work can still be found in education, parenting, and childcare.

ATTRIBUTION THEORY

Giving meaning to everything we do

The way in which a person attaches meaning to their behavior and to the behavior of others can be explained by attribution theory. In other words, how do we explain the events we are seeing and why do we do it? Essentially, attribution theory states that people explain the behavior of themselves and those around them by assigning attributes to this behavior.

Doctoral Definitions

ATTRIBUTE: An inference about what causes a particular behavior.

FRITZ HEIDER

A theory involving attribution was first proposed by Austrian psychologist Fritz Heider in 1958. Heider called it *naïve psychology* or "common sense," and thought that in order to make sense of the world, people seek to find cause-and-effect relationships.

His two main ideas about attribution were:

1. People look for internal attributions, like personality traits, mood, and attitudes, to explain the behavior of other people. For example, an individual might attribute jealousy to another person.
2. People make external attributions, like environmental or situational, to explain their own behavior.

EDWARD JONES AND KEITH DAVIS

In 1965, psychologists Edward Jones and Keith Davis created the correspondent inference theory. This theory helps explain the process of creating an internal attribution.

Jones and Davis believed that a person will pay particular attention to a behavior that is intentional—Jones and Davis called it "dispositional attribution"—and that these internal attributions provide us with enough information so that we can predict the individual's behavior in the future. For example, a person may make a connection between seeing someone act in a friendly manner and believing that individual to be a friendly person. This process of inferring that an individual's behavior corresponds with the personality of the individual is known as correspondent inference. Jones and Davis identified five sources that they believed led a person to make a correspondent inference:

1. **Choice:** Behavior that is freely chosen is the result of internal factors.
2. **Social Desirability:** When a behavior is nonconforming, a person will make internal

inferences more than they will make behaviors that are socially undesirable.

3. **Intentional vs. Accidental Behavior:** When a behavior is intentional, this means it is most likely attributed to the personality of the person, and when a behavior is accidental, it is most likely attributed to external or situational causes.
4. **Noncommon Effects:** If the behavior of another person leads to important results for yourself.
5. **Hedonistic Relevance:** If the behavior of another person seems to be directly intended to help or hurt you, it can be assumed that it is not simply a byproduct of the situation or event you and the other person are in, and that it is "personal."

HAROLD KELLEY

The most well-known attribution theory is Harold Kelley's covariation model of

1967. Kelley created a logical model to understand when an action could be an external attribution and when it could be an internal model.

Doctoral Definitions

COVARIATION: When an individual has information from many observations that occur in different situations and at different times.

Kelley stated there are three types of causal information that influence an individual's judgment and that these are taken into account when a person tries to figure out the cause of particular behaviors. When there is a low factor (behaviors do not conform and are low in desirability by others), this means it is an internal attribution.

1. **Consistency:** The degree to which a person acts a particular way every time a similar situation

occurs. For example, if someone only smokes cigarettes when he or she is out with his or her friends, there is a high consistency in behavior. If, however, a person only smokes cigarettes every now and then for a special occasion, there is a low consistency in behavior.

2. **Consensus:** The degree to which other people will act in a similar way when a similar situation occurs. For example, if one person smokes while drinking with a friend and his or her friend also smokes, then the behavior is high in consensus. If only the first person smokes, and the friend does not join in on the activity, then the behavior is low in consensus.
3. **Distinctiveness:** The degree to which an individual acts the same way in similar situations. If an individual only smokes cigarettes when he or she is with friends, then the behavior is high in distinctiveness, and if an individual

will smoke at any time in any place, then the behavior is low in distinctiveness.

BERNARD WEINER

Bernard Weiner's theory on attribution placed emphasis on achievement. Weiner stated that the most significant factors that affect attributions are effort, ability, luck, and the difficulty of the task. He classified attributions in three causal dimensions:

1. **Stability and instability:** Will the causes of the behavior change as time passes?
2. **Locus of control:** Internal vs. External. An internal locus of control is when an individual decides what to do on their own, while an external locus of control is when behavior is influenced by situational and external factors.
3. **Controllability:** Causes that an individual has the ability to control, like their own skill set, versus

causes that an individual does not have the ability to control, like luck or the actions of other people.

Weiner suggests that when an individual is successful, he or she tends to attribute his or her success internally to his or her skill set, but when someone else is successful, success is attributed externally to luck or circumstance. When an individual fails or is not successful, external attribution is commonly used, and instead of blaming him or herself, the cause will be attributed to situational or external factors. This is known as the self-serving bias. When other people are not successful or fail, however, an individual will commonly use internal attribution, believing it to be the result of internal factors.

ATTRIBUTIONAL BIASES AND ERRORS

Like the self-serving bias, there are several more examples of attributional biases and errors that people will commonly default to as they try to find a reason for behavior.

Fundamental Attribution Error

This is the tendency to underestimate external factors and overestimate internal factors when trying to explain the behavior of another individual. This is common when we don't know a person very well, or it may happen because of our tendency to focus more on the situation instead of the individual. For example, a student does not hand in an assignment and the teacher assumes this is because the student is lazy, without considering the student's situation.

Culture Bias

The people in North America and Western Europe tend to be more of an individualist culture, where individual values and goals are embraced, while the people in Latin America, Asia, and Africa tend to have more collectivist cultures, where family and conformity is embraced. People from individualist cultures will often make fundamental attribution errors and self-serving biases more than people from collectivist cultures; and people from collectivist cultures will often make self-effacing biases—the opposite of a self-serving bias, where success is attributed to external factors and failure is attributed to internal factors—more than people from individualist cultures.

Actor/Observer Difference

Even if an individual is in the same situation as another person, attribution can change depending on whether the person is the actor or the observer in the situation. For example, someone might justify doing poorly on a test by saying the teacher never went over the subject matter of a question. However, if others in the class did poorly and that individual did well, the individual might claim that it was because the rest of the class just didn't pay attention.

EMOTION

Why we feel the way we do

What exactly is emotion? In psychology, emotion is defined as a state of feeling that involves physiological and psychological changes that then influence the way a person thinks and behaves. There are three main categories that theories of emotion can be classified into:

- Neurological, which are based on the notion that brain activity will lead to an emotional response.
- Physiological, which are based on the notion that responses from the body are what create emotions.
- Cognitive, which are based on the notion that thinking and mental activity are responsible for emotions.

Some of the primary theories that psychologists have developed regarding emotion include:

THE JAMES-LANGE THEORY

The James-Lange theory, which was actually proposed independently by physiologist Carl Lange and psychologist William James in the 1920s, is one of the best-known theories on emotions. This theory suggests that all emotions are the result of a physiological reaction to events.

The James-Lange theory can be broken down as follows:

PROGRESSION OF EMOTION AS PHYSIOLOGICAL REACTIONS

If an individual witnesses an external stimulus, the result is a physiological reaction. From this physiological reaction comes a feeling of emotion, otherwise known as an emotional reaction, based on how the physical reaction has been interpreted.

For example, if you are walking along a path and you suddenly see a mountain lion facing you, your heart may begin to pound and your body may begin to tremble. According to the James-Lange theory, you will then interpret this physical reaction and reach the conclusion that you are scared.

There are many solid arguments that disprove the James-Lange theory, and it has mostly been abandoned by modern science. Psychologists, however, do still consider the James-Lange theory to be very influential; and there are even examples where this theory holds true, such as what happens to a person when he or she develops a phobia or panic disorder. If an individual experiences a physiological reaction, like getting sick in public, it can lead to an emotional reaction, like getting anxious, and an association can form between the two states. The person may then attempt to avoid any type of situation that would result in that emotion being triggered.

THE CANNON-BARD THEORY

Created by Walter Cannon and Philip Bard as an argument against the James-

Lange theory in the 1930s, the Cannon-Bard theory states physiological reactions and emotions are experienced simultaneously. According to the theory, emotions occur when the thalamus—the portion of the brain that is responsible for motor control, awake and sleep states, and sensory signals—sends the brain a message as a response to a particular stimulus. The result from this message being transmitted is a physiological reaction.

To break it down further, consider the following diagram:

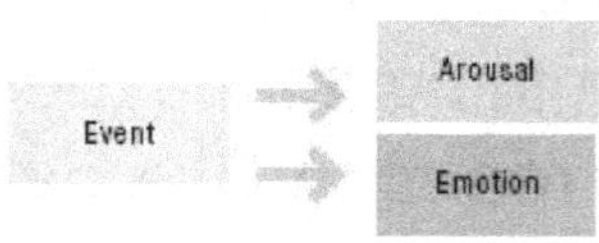

EVENTS TRIGGERING AROUSAL AND EMOTION

There is an original emotional stimulus that is taken in by sensory organs. The stimulus is then transmitted to the cortex to determine how the response will be directed, which in turn stimulates the thalamus. In other words, the stimulus is being perceived and interpreted. Then, two reactions occur simultaneously: the emotional reaction and the bodily reaction.

Returning to the earlier example, if you are walking along a path and see a mountain lion, you will experience the trembling and heart pounding simultaneously with the emotion of fear.

THE SCHACHTER-SINGER THEORY

The Schachter-Singer theory, created by Stanley Schachter and Jerome E. Singer in 1962, is an example of a cognitive theory. According to the Schachter-Singer Theory, which is also known as the two-factor theory, physiological arousal from an event is the first stage that occurs. Following the physiological arousal, an individual must then find the reason for why this arousal occurred, and it is only *after* this happens that the individual can characterize the experience and label it an emotion.

For example, when a woman is walking down an empty street late at night and suddenly hears footsteps behind her, she may start trembling and her heart rate may begin to increase. As the woman notices her physical response, she will come to the realization that she is by herself on the street. She will then begin to believe that she is in danger and experience the emotion of fear.

ALTERNATIVE VIEW OF EMOTIONAL RESPONSE

LAZARUS THEORY

Developed by Richard Lazarus in the 1990s, Lazarus's theory on emotion claims that before an emotion or physiological arousal can take place, a thought must occur first. Essentially, you have to consider the situation that you are in before any type of emotion can be experienced.

Take the example of walking down the empty street late at night. When a woman hears footsteps while walking down the street, the thought that she is in danger will occur first—for example, the thought that there is a mugger behind her—and as a result, her heart rate increases, her body begins trembling, and the emotion of fear is experienced.

Like the Cannon-Bard theory, the Lazarus theory involves emotion and physiological arousal occurring at the same time.

CONCURRENT EMOTION AND AROUSAL

FACIAL FEEDBACK THEORY

The origins of the facial feedback theory can be linked to the work of William James, and was further explored by Silvan Tomkins in 1962. This theory claims that emotion is actually the experience of facial muscle changes that occur. Otherwise, according to the theory, we are just thinking intellectually. So when a person smiles, it means that he or she is experiencing happiness, and when a person frowns, it means that he or she is experiencing sadness, and so on. These changes in our facial muscles are what prompt the brain into specifying a basis for emotion, instead of the other way around.

Once again, let's look at the scenario with the woman walking alone on a street at night. When she hears the footsteps coming from behind, her eyes will widen and her teeth will clench. The brain then interprets these changes in the facial muscles as expressing the emotion of fear, and therefore, the brain tells the woman that she is experiencing fear.

FACIAL CHANGES TRIGGERING EMOTION

Carney Landis's Facial Expressions Study

In 1924, a psychology graduate student at the University of Minnesota by the name of Carney Landis created an experiment to understand the relationship between facial expressions and emotions. Landis wanted to see if people shared universal facial expressions when certain emotions were evoked. For example, is the facial expression someone has for disgust the same as everyone else?

For his experiment, Landis used mostly fellow graduate students. Once inside of the lab, Landis painted black lines on the faces of the subjects so that he could easily follow any muscle movement. Each participant was then exposed to various stimuli that Landis chose in order to elicit a strong response. As each test subject responded, a photograph of his or her face was taken by Landis. The stimuli Landis used included making the subjects smell ammonia, look at pornography, and place their hands in a bucket full of frogs. The final part of the test, however, was the most disturbing.

In the final stage of the experiment, Landis presented a live rat to the subjects and told them they had to behead it. Even though every participant was disgusted by the notion, two-thirds actually did it. For the one-third of the participants that had refused to decapitate the rat, Landis did it for them.

While the Landis facial expressions experiment did little to show any universality among facial expression and its relation to emotion, it did anticipate the results that Stanley Milgram would have with his obedience studies, which would occur forty years later. Landis, however, was too focused on his work involving facial expressions to see that the compliance of his test subjects was the most interesting aspect of his study.

PERSONALITY
What makes you ... you?

When discussing personality, psychologists look at the thoughts, behaviors, and emotions that an individual has that make him or her unique—also known as a "mental system." Personality is individualized, and, for the most part, it will remain consistent throughout an individual's life. While there are many interpretations as to what constitutes personality, several key characteristics are generally accepted in the field of study:

- In general, there is a consistency and noticeable order to behavior. People behave in the same or similar ways in different types of situations.
- Personality influences how a person behaves and responds to their environment, and is also the

cause of behaving in particular ways.

- While personality is a psychological concept, biological processes have a large influence and impact on it.
- Behavior is not the only thing that displays personality. Personality can be seen in interactions with other people, relationships, thoughts, and emotions.

TRAIT THEORIES

There are several theories and schools of thought that try to understand how personality develops, and many have already been discussed in depth. These include humanist theories (such as Maslow's hierarchy of needs), which emphasize the role of free will and the experience of the individual; psychoanalytic theories (like the work of Sigmund Freud) that emphasize early experiences and the unconscious); behavioral theories (like classical and operant conditioning), which suggest that the individual and his or her interaction with the environment lead to the development of personality; and trait theories, which are particularly noteworthy because of their emphasis on the differences among people. Trait theories suggest personality is unique to an individual and made up of a combination of characteristics responsible for making a person behave in a particular way. These characteristics are known as traits. Trait theories, then, focus on finding and measuring the personality traits that comprise each individual. Throughout the history of psychology, there have been several trait theories. Among the most important are:

Allport's Trait Theory

In 1936, Harvard psychologist Gordon Allport, who also taught the very first personality psychology class in the United States, developed his trait theory of personality. Allport went through the dictionary and searched for every term he felt described a personality trait. With a list of over 4,500 words, Allport organized these traits into three categories:

1. **Cardinal traits:** Traits that control and define the entire personality of an individual. As a result, these types of traits are often synonymous with the individual, and are very rare. These traits include Christ-like, Narcissistic, and Machiavellian.
2. **Central traits:** Traits that are common. These include traits like friendliness, kindness, honesty, etc.
3. **Secondary traits:** Traits that appear under particular conditions and circumstances. For example, becoming nervous prior to giving a speech in public.

Cattell's Sixteen Personality Factors

Working off of Gordon Allport's theory, psychologist Raymond Cattell took Allport's list of more than 4,200 personality traits and dwindled it down to 171 traits, by combining those that were similar to one another and removing traits that were uncommon. Cattell then created questionnaires that used these traits and tested a large population sample.

Once Cattell had the results from the questionnaires, he identified any terms that were closely related and used a statistical process known as factor analysis to decrease the number of main personality traits even further. He concluded that a total of sixteen personality traits were the source of all personalities, and that every single person had these traits to some degree. The sixteen personality factors Cattell identified are:

- **Abstractedness:** Being imaginative and abstract versus being grounded and practical
- **Apprehension:** Being worried and insecure versus being confident and secure
- **Dominance:** Being forceful and assertive versus being submissive and obedient
- **Emotional stability:** Being calm versus being emotionally unstable and high-strung

- **Liveliness:** Being enthusiastic and spontaneous versus being restrained and serious
- **Openness to change:** Being flexible and open versus being traditional and attached to the familiar
- **Perfectionism:** Being self-disciplined and controlling versus being undisciplined and flexible
- **Privateness:** Being discreet and shrewd versus being open and unpretentious
- **Reasoning:** Thinking abstractly and being more intelligent versus thinking concretely and being less intelligent
- **Rule consciousness:** Being conscientious and conforming versus being nonconforming and disregarding rules
- **Self-reliance:** Being self-sufficient and individualistic versus being dependent
- **Sensitivity:** Being sentimental and tender-hearted versus being unsentimental and tough-minded

- **Social boldness:** Being uninhibited and venturesome versus being shy and timid
- **Tension:** Being impatient and frustrated versus being relaxed and placid
- **Vigilance:** Being suspicious and skeptical versus being trusting and accepting
- **Warmth:** Being outgoing and attentive to people versus being distant and reserved

EYSENCK'S THREE DIMENSIONS

Psychologist Hans Eysenck created a personality model in 1947 independent of other trait theories, and he updated the model in the late 1970s. His model was based on the notion that all people shared three universal traits:

1. **Introversion versus extraversion:** Introversion is when an individual directs his or her attention on inner experiences, which results in the individual

being quieter and more reserved. Extraversion is when an individual directs his or her attention outward to people around them and to the environment. Someone who is high in extraversion will be more outgoing and sociable.

2. **Neuroticism versus emotional stability:** According to Eysenck, neuroticism relates to one's propensity to get emotional or become upset, while emotional stability relates to one's propensity to stay emotionally constant.
3. **Psychoticism:** Individuals high in psychoticism will have hostile, antisocial, manipulative, and apathetic tendencies and will find dealing with reality to be difficult.

THE BIG FIVE PERSONALITY TRAITS

Personality theorists today believe that there were too many personality traits in Cattell's theory, and not enough personality traits in Eysenck's theory.

Instead, many believe a theory known as the "Big Five." This model claims that the basis of personality comes from the interaction of five main traits. These traits are:

1. **Extraversion:** The level of an individual's sociability.
2. **Agreeableness:** The level of an individual's friendliness, affection, trust, and positive social behavior.
3. **Conscientiousness:** The level of an individual's organization, thoughtfulness, and impulse control.
4. **Neuroticism:** The level of an individual's emotional stability.
5. **Openness:** The level of an individual's imagination, creativity, and range of interests.

While there are many different theories that approach the subject of personality in very different ways, one thing is certain among them all: Personality is an extremely important topic. It generally remains consistent throughout one's life, and is responsible for making every single individual think, behave, and feel in a unique and individualized way.

LEADERSHIP THEORIES

What does it take to become a leader?

In the early twentieth century, interest in theories about leadership began to flourish in the world of psychology as the Great Depression and World War II made people start to wonder what it took to be a good leader. While early theories focused on the qualities that make up a leader versus the qualities that make up a follower, later leadership theories focused on levels of skill and situational factors.

While there are many different theories regarding leadership, there are eight major types that these theories can be classified as:

GREAT MAN THEORIES

The main idea behind the great man theories of leadership is that the ability to become a leader is inherent, and that there are certain people that are naturally born to be leaders.

The great man theory was originally proposed by historian Thomas Carlyle. During the nineteenth century, when this theory was most popular, some argued that the existence of such men as Mahatma Gandhi, Abraham Lincoln, Alexander the Great, and Julius Caesar provided support for the validity of this argument—it just seemed like the right man emerged from nowhere to lead.

CONTINGENCY THEORIES

Contingency theories claim the ability to lead is dependent upon situational factors. These factors include, but are not limited to, the favored style of the leader and the behaviors and abilities of the people following the leader.

Contingency theories claim that there is no single style of leadership that is universally effective, and that one style of leadership may work better under particular circumstances than other styles of leadership. This means that leaders that are very effective in one environment may be completely unsuccessful if placed in another environment.

TRAIT THEORIES

Trait theories, like the great man theories, are based on the assumption that people are born with particular traits that make them well-suited to become a leader. Trait theories attempt to identify and compare key personality and behavioral traits that leaders share.

One of the difficulties that arises in discussing the trait theory of leadership is the problem of how two individuals with otherwise similar traits end up in completely divergent leadership positions. One may become a great leader and one may remain a follower, or even become a failed leader, despite sharing many of the same outward traits.

SITUATIONAL THEORIES

Situational theories are based on the idea that leaders choose the best course of action to take depending upon the situational factors. Situational theories claim that leaders should not utilize just one single style of leading; but rather, leaders should take all situational factors into account. The situational factors include the capability of individuals who are followers and the motivation of the leader.

Among other factors, it is the perception that the leader has of the situation and his or her followers, as well as the leader's mood and perception of him or herself, that affects what the leader will eventually do.

PARTICIPATIVE THEORIES

The main idea behind participative leadership theories is that an ideal leader takes into consideration the input of other people. In this type of leadership, participation and contributions are encouraged. This process not only makes other people feel engaged and relevant in the decision-making process, but they also feel more committed to it as well.

It should be noted that in participative theories, even though there is participation from followers, it is up to the leader to give that right to other people.

BEHAVIORAL THEORIES

In contrast to great man theories and trait theories, behavior theories are based on the notion that a leader is not born, but made, and that leadership does not come about through mental characteristics. Instead, behavioral theories claim leadership is something that can be learned by observation and teaching. Leadership, according to behavioral theories, is a learnable behavior.

TRANSFORMATIONAL THEORIES

Transformational theories, which are also called relationship theories, focus on the relationship between a leader and his or her followers. According to transformational leadership theories, a leader will make followers understand the significance and benefits of a task by motivating and inspiring his or her followers. In transformational leadership, focus is not only placed on the performance of the group, but also on making sure every individual has reached his or her fullest potential. As a result, leadership that follows this type of theory also features high moral and ethical standards.

TRANSACTIONAL THEORIES

Transactional theories, which are also called management theories, emphasize the role of the supervisor, performance of the group, and organization. In transactional theories, leadership is based on a system made up of rewards and punishments, and expectations of followers are clearly understood. Transactional theories of leadership are commonly seen in the workplace. If an employee is successful, they will be rewarded, and if an employee fails, they will be punished or reprimanded.

What does it take to make a great leader? Is it something you are born with? Is it just based on the particular situation at hand? Does listening to the input of others make you any better? Is good leadership a learned behavior?

Perhaps it occurs by making the followers understand what it takes to reach their highest potential, or maybe a good leader is born out of creating a system of rewards and punishments. Understanding leadership theories and how others respond to forms of leadership can have very real applications in the world. But how does one make a great leader? To put it simply: many different ways.

DREAMS

What goes on when the lights are off

In psychology, dreams are defined as any thoughts, images, or emotions that a person experiences while asleep. Psychologists have yet to agree on why we dream and what these dreams mean, but there are several significant theories.

The "Science" of Sleep

Believe it or not, scientists still don't know the reason or purpose for sleeping in the first case!

FREUD'S PSYCHOANALYTIC THEORY OF DREAMS

Sigmund Freud believed that the contents of our dreams were associated with wish fulfillment, and that our dreams represented the thoughts, motivations, and desires of our unconscious.

Furthermore, Freud believed that the sexual instincts that the conscious represses appear in our dreams. In Freud's book, *The Interpretation of Dreams*, Freud broke dreams down into two components:

- **Manifest content**—The actual thoughts, content, and images in the dream
- **Latent content**—The psychological meaning in the dream that is hidden

To understand the meaning behind dreams, Freud broke dreams down into five distinct parts:

- **Displacement:** When a desire for something is represented by something or someone else
- **Projection:** When the wants and desires of the dreamer are pushed onto another person in the dream
- **Symbolization:** When the urges and desires that are suppressed

are metaphorically acted out in the dream

- **Condensation:** When a lot of information is compressed into one image or thought, making meaning difficult to decipher
- **Secondary Revision:** The final stage of dreaming, where the incoherent elements become reorganized into a comprehensible dream

While research has refuted Freud's theory of the latent content being disguised by the manifest content, the work of Sigmund Freud contributed greatly to interest in the field of dream interpretation.

CARL JUNG'S THEORY ON DREAMS

While Jung believed in much of what Freud did when it came to dreams, Jung thought dreams were not just an expression of repressed desires, but that they also compensated for those parts of the psyche that were underdeveloped during waking life. Jung also believed dreams revealed the collective unconscious and personal unconscious, and featured archetypes that were representative of unconscious thoughts.

THE ACTIVATION-SYNTHESIS MODEL OF DREAMING

In 1977, Robert McCarley and J. Allan Hobson created the activation-synthesis model, in which they proposed that dreams were caused by the physiological processes of the brain.

According to the activation-synthesis model, during the final stage of the sleep cycle known as rapid eye movement (REM) sleep, circuits within the brain stem activate, which in turn activates parts of the limbic system that play a key role in memory, sensation, and emotion. The brain then attempts to produce meaning from this internal activity, resulting in dreams.

When the activation-synthesis model came out, it was met with controversy within the field of psychology, and particularly among those who followed Freud's teachings. While many psychologists were attempting to find the hidden meaning behind dreams, the activation-synthesis model proposed that these dreams were simply the product of the brain trying to process brain activity.

Hobson did not think dreams were utterly meaningless, however, and claimed instead that dreams were the "most creative conscious state," where new ideas, both fanciful and useful, are formed.

HALL'S THEORY ON DREAMS

Psychologist Calvin S. Hall claimed the goal of dream interpretation was to understand the individual doing the dreaming, and not to simply understand the dream itself.

Hall claimed that properly interpreting dreams required understanding several items:

- The actions the dreamer partakes in within the dream

- Any figures or objects that appear in the dream
- All of the interactions that occur between the dreamer and characters within the dream
- The setting of the dream
- Any transitions that occur within the dream
- The outcome of the dream

DOMHOFF'S THEORY ON DREAMS

G. William Domhoff studied under Calvin Hall, and came to the conclusion that dreams are actually reflections of any thoughts or concerns that occur during the waking life of the individual dreaming. According to Domhoff's theory, dreams are the result of neurological processes.

COMMON THEMES FOUND IN DREAMS

The following are ten of the most common themes people experience while dreaming, as well as the possible meanings of these themes according to Freudian theory.

1. **Taking a test that you are not prepared for:** This type of dream does not only pertain to an academic test, and will usually be specific to the dreamer. For example, an actor might dream about not remembering their audition or not being able to recognize the words on a script. This type of dream deals with the feeling of being exposed, and the test might symbolize being judged or evaluated by someone else.
2. **Being naked or inappropriately dressed in public:** This type of dream relates to feelings of shame or vulnerability.
3. **Being chased or attacked:** This type of dream is much more common in children, whose dreams tend to focus on more physical rather than social fears. Additionally, their size can often

make them feel as though they are more physically vulnerable. In adults, this type of dream can be a sign of being under stress.

4. **Falling:** Falling can represent feelings of being extremely overwhelmed with your current situation and having a loss of control.
5. **Being lost in transit:** This often represents feeling lost, or trying to get something or find your path and being unsure of how to do it.
6. **Losing a tooth:** This can represent feeling unheard or unseen in a personal relationship, or feelings of aggression.
7. **Natural disasters:** This can signify feeling so overwhelmed by personal problems that it seems they are raging out of control.
8. **Flying:** This can represent a desire to escape or be free from a situation.
9. **Dying or being injured:** This can represent something in the

dreamer's everyday life that no longer thrives or is wilting away, like a personal relationship or personal attribute, and does not necessarily mean or imply true thoughts of death.

10. **Losing control of a car:** This type of dream can result from feelings of stress and fear, and of not feeling in control of everyday life.

While psychologists still do not fully understand dreams, their interpretation plays a key role in modern psychology. From Freud's prominently used interpretation of dream analysis, which suggests dreams are connected to our unconscious and represent repressed desires, to the work of G. William Domhoff, who believed dreams were merely a result of neurological processes, understanding why dreams occur and the various details and possible meanings behind them remains a very important part of psychology.

ART THERAPY
The art of getting better

Art is an extremely expressive medium. It can help people communicate, aid in dealing with stress, and can let someone discover and study the different parts of their own personality. In psychology, art is used to improve a person's mental health and can even be used to treat psychological disorders. This is referred to as art therapy.

By integrating the creative process that is required to create art with psychotherapeutic techniques, art therapy can allow an individual to resolve their problems, decrease the amount of stress they face in their life, manage their behavior, improve their interpersonal skills, and strengthen their self-awareness and self-control.

Art therapy first began to emerge as a distinct form of therapy in the 1940s, when psychiatrists took interest in the paintings created by mentally ill patients and educators began to realize that developmental, cognitive, and emotional growth could be seen in the artwork of children.

WHEN TO USE ART THERAPY

There are groups of people who have been shown to respond very positively to art therapy. Some of these groups include:

- Adults that are struggling with severe stress
- Children that are struggling with learning disabilities
- People who have undergone a traumatic experience
- People that have mental health problems
- People that are struggling from a brain injury
- Children that are struggling with social problems and behavioral problems at home or at school
- Anyone suffering from depression, anxiety, or domestic abuse

What Art Therapy Isn't

Art therapy is *not* a recreational activity or a time to teach someone how to make art, and no previous experience in art is needed for an individual to partake in this type of therapy. Most importantly, art therapy does not involve the therapist interpreting the patient's artwork. Art therapy is about teaching someone how to heal through his or her art.

HOW ART THERAPY WORKS

Art methods involved in art therapy include painting, drawing, collage, and sculpture. Once in an environment that makes the patient feel safe, an art therapist will either provide the topic for the patient to work from, or the patient will be invited to work without any direction.

As the patient creates art pertaining to their life experiences or an event, the process of making art allows the patient to think about their experience on a deeper level and transform what is in their head into symbols and metaphors.

By making these unique symbols and metaphors, the patient is able to now define these images on their own terms, which is an important part of recovery and self-discovery. The patient is the only person who knows and has the ability to explain what these symbols represent.

This process of taking an experience from the person's "inner-self" and putting it out into the world as a physical object helps the individual become distant to the experience, which in turn makes him or her feel safer about talking about what he or she has made. So instead of having to speak about their problems directly, which can be very difficult for them to do, they can talk to the therapist about the artwork they have made. Gradually, this process increases a person's understanding, self-acceptance, and self-awareness.

OTHER BENEFITS FROM ART THERAPY

Along with increasing self-awareness and self-acceptance, there are many other benefits that an individual can gain from art therapy. These include:

- Being forced to actively participate in the process, which fights boredom, alienation, and feelings of apathy
- Decision-making and choices are encouraged
- Creativity is nurtured, and this can then allow an individual to react differently towards situations that may be difficult
- Catharsis, a cleansing of negative feelings, can occur
- Interpersonal and social learning can occur

Not Just Painting

There are also versions of art therapy in music, dance, writing, drama (known as creative art therapy), and even the performing arts (known as expressive art therapy).

What is truly exceptional about art therapy is that an individual has the ability to take an active role in the therapeutic process. By expressing thoughts through artwork and symbols, a person can recover and become self-aware on his or her own terms.

HYPNOSIS

It's not smoke and mirrors

In psychology, hypnosis is a technique used during therapy that involves a patient going into a very deep state of relaxation so that the individual can really begin to concentrate on his or her mind. During this state, connections between what the individual is thinking, feeling, and doing become clearer.

While hypnosis is often portrayed negatively in the media, it has actually been clinically proven to provide not only therapeutic benefits, but medical benefits as well. The method is particularly effective when it comes to reduction of anxiety and pain, and some even believe that it can be useful in reducing symptoms related to dementia.

Most of the time, hypnosis is used as an aid to the therapeutic process, and is not the treatment itself.

HOW HYPNOSIS WORKS

Hypnosis provides care and treatment by altering and reprogramming an individual's subconscious mind. When placed under hypnosis, the conscious mind of an individual is subdued, while the subconscious mind is awakened. In order for there to be any real change in the person's life, many psychologists believe that the subconscious mind, not merely the conscious mind, needs to change. Because the subconscious mind is more present during hypnosis than the conscious mind, thoughts, feelings, and memories that were once hidden can be explored.

For example, if a person wants to quit smoking, he or she may do everything in his or her power on a conscious level to try and stop, but there may still be a desire from the subconscious mind that contributes to failed attempts at quitting. By understanding, changing, and reprogramming the subconscious mind, the individual may finally be able to succeed because the subconscious mind has been altered.

When being hypnotized, a patient is not put into a deep sleep and cannot be forced to do anything against their better judgment or something they wouldn't otherwise do; nor does a patient have to follow every command that the therapist says. Instead, the person being hypnotized is constantly aware of his or her environment and situation.

Two Methods of Hypnotic Therapy

PATIENT ANALYSIS: Using hypnosis to find the underlying cause of a symptom or disorder, such as a past trauma or event, that is hidden in the unconscious mind. Once revealed, the problem can be further attended to in psychotherapy.

SUGGESTION THERAPY: Once hypnotized, a person will be able to change a specific behavior, like smoking or nail-biting, because they will respond to suggestions better. This technique can also be used to alter sensations and perceptions, and is frequently used in pain management.

WHAT CAN BE TREATED WITH HYPNOSIS

Because hypnosis can help a person deal with anything they find hard to handle, there are many mental, emotional, and physical conditions that hypnosis can help treat. Common conditions that hypnosis is used for include:

- Phobias
- Stress and anxiety
- Panic attacks
- Grief
- Eating disorders
- Sleep disorders
- Depression
- Addiction
- Weight loss
- Smoking cessation
- Symptoms of ADHD
- Reducing pain during childbirth
- Sexual problems
- Reducing nausea and vomiting in patients that suffer from cancer and are undergoing chemotherapy
- Easing symptoms of Irritable Bowel Syndrome

ALBERT ELLIS (1913–2007)

Founder of a new type of psychotherapy

Albert Ellis was born on September 27th, 1913, in Pittsburgh, Pennsylvania. Ellis described his relationship with his parents as distant, and his mother struggled with bipolar disorder. As a result, Ellis cared for and raised his younger brother and sister.

In 1934, Ellis graduated from the City University of New York and began writing about sexuality when he first took an interest in psychology. From there, Ellis attended Columbia University, where he would receive both his MA in clinical psychology (1943) and his PhD (1947). Ellis was originally a strong proponent of Sigmund Freud's psychoanalysis. However, the works of Karen Horney, Alfred Adler, and Erich Fromm had a great influence on Ellis, and soon he began questioning, and ultimately severing ties with, Freud's work.

Instead of following Freud's concepts, Ellis created his own form of psychotherapy, which he named Rational Therapy—this would later be referred to as Rational Emotive Behavior Therapy (REBT). This therapy is commonly seen as the beginning of cognitive behavioral therapy. In 1959, Ellis founded the Institute for Rational Living.

Ellis was extremely active during the sexual revolution of the 1960s, and was an outspoken atheist. It was only after working on REBT with numerous religious practitioners that Ellis could finally see the psychological benefits that a belief in a higher being could bring to people. While he never stopped being an atheist, his outspokenness diminished, and Ellis came to the conclusion that having the choice could allow for the highest psychological result.

While much of Ellis's early work was met with criticism, in the last half of his life he received great praise as cognitive behavioral therapies were increasingly recognized as effective methods of treatment. Today, Albert Ellis is considered to be one of the most important people in the field of psychology. Albert Ellis died on July 24th, 2007.

THE ABC MODEL

In Albert Ellis' concept of Rational Emotive Behavior Therapy, he believed that events occur every day that prompt a person to observe and interpret what is going on. These interpretations then turn into particular beliefs that the person will form concerning the event. These beliefs will also include the person's role in the event. Once a belief has been developed, an emotional consequence is experienced as a result of that belief. Here is a helpful visual illustration of this concept:

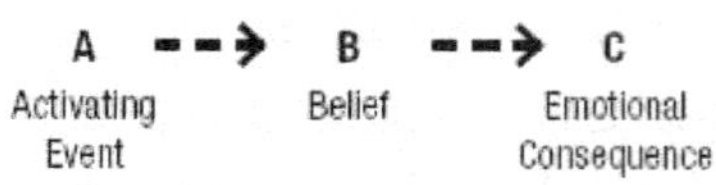

ACTIVATING EVENTS AND EMOTIONAL CONSEQUENCES

1. **A:** Your superior falsely accuses you of stealing from him and threatens to have you fired
2. **B:** You react, "How dare he? He has no reason to accuse me!"
3. **C:** You feel mad

Ellis's ABC attempts to show that event B is what causes event C to occur, and that it is not A that directly causes C. You are not mad because you have been falsely accused and threatened to lose your job; you are mad because of the belief that occurs in B.

Doctoral Definitions

Cognitive behavioral therapy: A type of psychotherapy where an individual works with a psychotherapist for a limited amount of sessions, and in a very structured way, so that the individual can begin to understand what feelings and thoughts influence their behavior.

THE THREE BASIC MUSTS

Ellis claims that there are three upsetting, irrational beliefs that we all share, no matter how different our expressions may be. Within each belief, there is a demand, which may either be about yourself, about other people, or about the world. These three common beliefs are referred to as the three basic musts.

1. A person must do well and win the approval of other people for his or her actions or else that individual is no good.
2. Others must treat you kindly, fairly, and thoughtfully, and in the precise way you want to be treated. If that does not happen, then those other people are no good and deserve punishment or condemnation.
3. A person must get what they want, when they want it, and they must not get something they do not want. If a person does not get what they want, then it is awful and they can't stand it.

The first belief will often lead to feelings of anxiety, depression, guilt, and embarrassment. The second belief will often lead to feelings of passive-aggression, anger, and violence. The third belief will often lead to procrastination and feelings of pity for oneself. While beliefs that are flexible and not demanding can result in healthy behavior and emotion, when these beliefs are demanding, problems and neuroses can begin to arise.

THE ROLE OF DISPUTING

The main idea behind Ellis's Rational Emotive Behavior Therapy is to help turn the patient's beliefs that are irrational into beliefs that are rational. This is done by having the therapist dispute the irrational beliefs of the patient. For example, a therapist might ask their client, "Why must others treat you kindly?" As the patient attempts to answer this question, they will slowly come to the realization that there is no rational reason for why these beliefs must occur.

THE THREE INSIGHTS

Ellis believed that everyone has the tendency to think irrationally, but the frequency, length, and intensity can be reduced with the use of three insights:

1. People do not simply get upset, but will become so as a result of having inflexible beliefs.
2. No matter what the reason is for getting upset, people continue to feel that way because they don't let go of their irrational beliefs.
3. The only way one can improve is by working hard to change these beliefs. This takes a lot of practice.

ACCEPTANCE OF REALITY

For a person to be emotionally healthy, they must accept reality, even if this reality is unpleasant. In REBT, therapists try to help a person reach three different types of acceptance:

1. **Unconditional self-acceptance:** An individual has

to accept that they are fallible, there is no reason for not having flaws, and they are no more or less worthy than anyone else.

2. **Unconditional other-acceptance:** An individual has to accept that he or she will be treated unfairly by other people sometimes, that there is no reason that other people have to treat him or her with fairness, and that people who treat him or her unfairly are no more or less worthy than anyone else.
3. **Unconditional life-acceptance:** An individual has to accept that life does not always work out the way they had hoped it would, that there is no reason for life to go the way they hoped it should, and that life, while it may be unpleasant at times, is never fully awful and is bearable.

Albert Ellis's Rational Emotive Behavior Therapy is currently one of the most popular forms of therapy today, and paved the way for all types of cognitive behavioral therapy.

COGNITIVE BEHAVIORAL THERAPY

Becoming aware of negative behavior

Cognitive behavioral therapy, which is commonly used to treat disorders like depression, phobias, anxiety, and addiction, is a form of psychotherapeutic treatment that focuses on changing negative behavior by altering the influential thoughts and feelings an individual has. In cognitive behavioral therapy, it is believed that thoughts and feelings actually influence and reinforce the behavior of a person.

For example, according to cognitive behavioral therapy, if a person is constantly thinking about car accidents, this will influence his or her behavior and he or she may avoid ever getting into a car or driving. If someone thinks negatively about their self-image and abilities, he or she will have a low self-esteem and, as a result, he or she may avoid social situations or miss out on opportunities.

By changing the thought patterns of an individual, his or her behavior will also change. Cognitive behavioral therapy focuses on helping an individual with a very specific problem that he or she is suffering from; and for this reason, it is often a short-term process. With cognitive behavioral therapy, the individual will begin to learn that while he or she may not be able to control everything that goes on he or she does in the outside world, he or she does have the ability to control how to approach and interpret things happening in his or her own environment.

THE STAGES OF COGNITIVE BEHAVIORAL THERAPY

Cognitive behavioral therapy can be broken down into two stages. The first stage of cognitive behavioral therapy is known as functional analysis. During this stage, a cognitive behavior therapist helps the individual identify which of his or her beliefs are problematic. It is at this time that the therapist understands what situations, feelings, and thoughts contribute to the individual's maladaptive behavior. While this stage may be difficult for a patient, the resulting insight and self-discovery is crucial to the process.

The second stage of cognitive behavioral therapy is dedicated to the specific behaviors. During this stage, an individual will begin to learn and rehearse new skills that he or she can then apply to the real world. This is usually a gradual process where an individual progressively works towards his or her goal. As each new step is introduced, the main goal will seem less daunting and more achievable.

MULTIMODAL THERAPY

A common form of cognitive behavioral therapy (other than the previously mentioned Rational Emotive Behavior Therapy) is Arnold Lazarus's Multimodal Therapy, which incorporates all of the characteristics of personality into the therapy, instead of simply concentrating on one or two elements.

Lazarus's Multimodal Therapy was built on the premise that all people are biological beings that experience certain modalities. These modalities are the ability to experience emotions, imagine, think, feel, smell, act, and relate to other people.

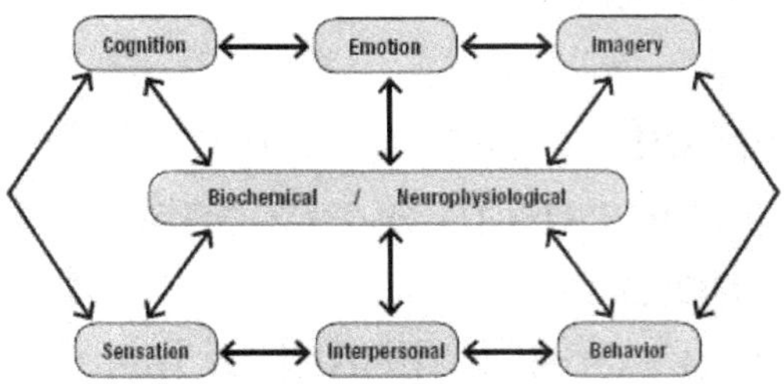

LAZARUS'S CONCEPTION OF MODALITIES

Lazarus listed these modalities under the acronym "BASIC I.D."

- Behavior
- Affective reactions or emotions
- Sensory reactions, like hearing, touching, seeing, smelling, and tasting

- Imagery, including self-image, thinking in images, and others
- Cognition, including beliefs, opinions, attitudes, thinking with words, and more
- Interpersonal, or how people communicate with other people
- Drugs and biology, including medications, health, exercise, sleep, diet, and more

The specific treatment in multimodal therapy is unique to every patient. Prior to starting therapy, an individual will complete a consultation that helps the therapist understand which modalities are being neglected and which are being prioritized by the individual. Therapy will then begin by focusing on the modality that will be the most beneficial to the patient. Eventually, however, there will be interventions with all of the modalities.

Doctoral Definitions

BRIDGING: Before the therapist can explore other modalities that may be more productive, they must first relate with the preferred modality of the individual.

TRACKING: Understanding, evaluating, and prioritizing the "firing order" of the modalities for the patient. People will usually react to situations in a pattern, and this is especially true if the situations are similar. Understanding what the patient's particular pattern is will be crucial for the treatment to be beneficial.

Multimodal therapy is also particularly noteworthy because it exhibits technical eclecticism, meaning a therapist can use a variety of techniques and psychotherapeutic approaches, and are not restricted to particular theoretical bases.

COGNITIVE THERAPY

Created by psychologist Aaron Beck in the 1960s, cognitive therapy is another popular form of cognitive behavioral therapy.

In cognitive therapy, it is believed that information is constantly being filtered and interpreted, and that this process leads to errors, false beliefs, and negative emotions. There are ten recognized patterns of faulty thinking, and these are referred to as cognitive distortions. In order to change the way you behave, you have to first change your thought processes, which can be done by understanding and fixing the cognitive distortions that apply to you. The ten cognitive distortions are:

1. **Overgeneralization:** Using an isolated situation and broadly assuming all others are the same way.
2. **Disqualifying the positive:** Acting as if events that are positive do not count.
3. **All-or-nothing thinking:** Only thinking in terms of absolutes and

not recognizing there can be middle ground.

4. **Emotional reasoning:** Instead of looking at a situation objectively by studying the facts, a person lets his or her emotions govern his or her thoughts on the situation.
5. **Jumping to conclusions:** Assuming the worst even when there is not sufficient evidence to back that claim.
6. **Magnification and Minimization:** Downplaying events that are positive, and paying a significant amount of attention to events that are negative.
7. **Mental filter:** Overlooking any positive events that occur in life, and mentally singling out the bad events.
8. **Should statements:** Instead of attempting to deal with how things currently are, one focuses on how things should be.
9. **Personalization:** Blaming oneself for things that are not

within one's control.

10. **Labeling and Mislabeling:** Giving false and cruel labels to other people and to oneself.

According to cognitive behavior therapy, one must change a negative thought process in order to change a negative behavior. Through approaches like Rational Emotive Behavior Therapy, cognitive therapy, and Multimodal Therapy, patients can come to understand and fight their negative thinking patterns, and then learn new skills necessary to combat the negative behavior.

HEURISTICS

Making decisions

Heuristics are the quick mental strategies that people use to solve problems. These are often referred to as “rule of thumb” strategies, and they allow for a person to make a fast and efficient decision without having to stop and deliberate over what the next course of action will be. Even though heuristics are oftentimes very helpful, they can also lead to errors, which are referred to as biases. In 1974, Daniel Kahneman and Amos Tversky identified what they considered to be the three major forms of heuristics, a designation that we still apply to this day.

AVAILABILITY HEURISTICS

Availability heuristics help people judge the probability or likelihood of an event occurring by using examples based on what they can remember. This can often lead to biases because instead of relying on complete data to make a judgment about likelihood, a person relies solely on his or her memories. Scientists believe that events that are recalled easily and quickly are often the most recent.

For example, if an individual watches the news and sees several stories about home foreclosures, he or she may believe that in general, there is a high probability of home foreclosure occurring; or if an individual can quickly provide examples of friends that are getting divorced, he or she may claim the divorce rate is higher, regardless of what actual statistics might say.

The availability heuristic can also make people overestimate the likelihood of events that are improbable—they may worry about flying after seeing an article on a recent plane crash. Conversely, they might underestimate the likelihood of other events that are probable—for example, people may feel that their likelihood of getting an STD from unprotected sex is low because their friends have had unprotected sex and don't have an STD, even though they are actually at high risk.

ANCHORING AND ADJUSTMENT

Anchoring and adjustment heuristics are based on the notion that people will often base their decisions or estimates on "anchors," or reference points. These anchors are pieces of information that are retrieved from the memory of the person, and they are adjusted in an attempt to fit the criteria of the decision. For example, you are asked the following:

Is the Mississippi River greater or less than 2,000 miles? Is it greater or less than 5,000 miles?

By answering the first part of the question, you have been provided an anchor by which to answer the other question; and as a result, you will base your second answer off of this anchor.

REPRESENTATIVENESS HEURISTICS

The representativeness heuristic describes how people will often determine the probability of an event or outcome by looking for a known event that they can compare it to, and then assuming that the probabilities will be the same. In the representativeness heuristic, the largest mistake is the assumption that a similarity in one thing will result in similarities in other things.

For example, if a person sees a man with arms covered in tattoos wearing a leather jacket, the person may use the representativeness heuristic and assume that this man is more likely to drive a motorcycle. The person believes this man is representative of what a motorcycle driver is, and groups the man into this category.

The representativeness heuristic can also be used to explain "gambler's fallacy," where people incorrectly assume that they have the ability to predict random events or a winning streak or losing streak based on previous information, even though the probability of the event occurring is the same. For example, if a coin is tossed several times, always lands heads-up, and a person claims that the next toss will surely land tails-up because it has landed heads-up too many times, they have completely disregarded the fact that there is a 50 percent chance it could land either way. The representativeness heuristic also makes people ignore base rates, the frequency of an event occurring.

HARRY STACK SULLIVAN (1892–1949)

Interpersonal psychoanalysis

Harry Stack Sullivan was born on February 21st, 1892, in Norwich, New York. The son of Irish immigrants, Sullivan grew up in a town with anti-Catholic sentiments, which left Sullivan feeling isolated socially—a situation that would later lead to the development of the concept of "social isolation" in his work.

In 1917, Sullivan earned his MD from the Chicago College of Medicine and Surgery. Sullivan is most known for his work in interpersonal relationships, and loneliness among those suffering from mental illnesses, his work with people suffering from schizophrenia, and his modifications to the work of Sigmund Freud. While Sullivan believed in Freud's main tenets, his approach towards psychoanalysis began to drift away from

Freud's—most significantly, from Freud's concept of psychosexual development.

From 1925 to 1929, Harry Stack Sullivan worked extensively with schizophrenics without the use of any medication and had great success. Sullivan claimed that the condition was not incurable, and that schizophrenia was largely the result of cultural forces. All of the men involved in this study were gay, which was perhaps particularly noteworthy for Sullivan, who many believe lived his entire life as a closeted gay man. Indeed, one of the patients from this study would later become Sullivan's lover and move in with him, though the gentleman was always referred to as his adopted son.

In 1933 and 1936, Sullivan helped found the William Alanson White Psychiatric Foundation and the Washington School of Psychiatry, respectively. Following World War II, Sullivan helped found the World Federation for Mental Health; and in 1938, he founded and became the editor of the journal, *Psychiatry*. On January 14th, 1949, Harry Stack Sullivan died. He was fifty-six years old. Sullivan's work in personality and psychotherapeutic techniques continues to influence the world of psychology.

HARRY STACK SULLIVAN'S INTERPERSONAL THEORY

While he lived a life largely in isolation, Harry Stack Sullivan understood the significance that interpersonal relations could have on an individual. Sullivan believed that personality was primarily the result of the relationships people have with one another. Sullivan viewed personality as a system of energy, comprised of either actual actions, which he called energy transformations, or the potential for actions, which he called tension. Sullivan identified two types of tensions: needs and anxiety.

Needs

In order to reduce needs, a certain action is required. Needs are related to particular zones of a person, like the genitals or mouth, or the general well-being of an individual. Needs are either physiological, like the need for food and oxygen, or interpersonal, like the need for intimacy and tenderness.

Anxiety

Anxiety cannot be relieved by consistent actions. This, Sullivan claimed, is the main force of disruption for interpersonal relationships. If anxiety and tensions are completely absent from an individual, then that individual is experiencing euphoria.

DYNAMISMS

Sullivan referred to a standard pattern of behavior as a dynamism, and believed that dynamisms could relate to tensions or to particular zones of the body. Sullivan identified four dynamisms:

- **Intimacy:** A close personal relationship amongst two individuals who are equal in status. This decreases loneliness and anxiety, and encourages interpersonal development.

- **Lust:** This is a self-centered desire that can be fulfilled without an intimate interpersonal relationship. Lust is a dynamism based entirely on sexual gratification, and does not necessarily require another individual for this need to be satisfied.
- **Malevolence:** Hatred, evil, and the feeling that you are living among your enemies define this dynamism. Children that are malevolent will have difficulty with intimacy and the ability to give and receive tenderness.
- **Self-System:** This is a pattern of behaviors that maintain an individual's interpersonal security and protect an individual from anxiety. This type of dynamism will commonly suppress any change in personality. If our self-system experiences anything inconsistent, security operations (psychological actions with the purpose of reducing interpersonal tensions) become necessary. Security

operations include things like dissociation, where an individual will block experiences from his or her awareness, and selective inattention, where an individual will block specific experiences from his or her awareness.

PERSONIFICATIONS

According to Harry Stack Sullivan, people develop personifications of themselves through interactions with other people. These personifications are:

- **Bad-Me:** These are aspects of one's self that are hidden from the rest of the world, and possibly one's self, because they are considered to be negative. Often, when we experience anxiety, it is because the bad-me is being recognized by the consciousness. For example, when a person recalls an action that resulted in embarrassment.
- **Good-Me:** This is everything that an individual enjoys about him or

herself. The good-me does not create anxiety, is shared with other people, and as a result, is oftentimes what an individual will choose to focus on.

- **Not-Me:** This is all of the things that create such anxiety that they are actually pushed into the unconsciousness so as to be kept out of our awareness.

Much like Sigmund Freud, Harry Stack Sullivan believed childhood experiences and the role of the mother play a key role in the development of an individual's personality. However, unlike Freud, Sullivan believed that personality can develop after adolescence and into adulthood. Sullivan referred to his developmental stages as "epochs," and believed that people pass through these epochs in a particular order that is dictated not by timing, but by the social environment of the individual. Sullivan's developmental epochs are:

- **Infancy (birth–one year):** During this epoch, the mother figure gives the child tenderness and the child learns anxiety.
- **Childhood (one–five years):** The mother remains the main interpersonal relationship with the child, but is now distinguished from other people that care for the child.
- **Juvenile (six–eight years):** The child begins to need playmates, or peers of the same status. This is the beginning of socialization, and a child should learn how to cooperate, compromise, and compete with other children.
- **Preadolescence (nine–twelve years):** This is the most important stage because any mistakes that were made before this epoch can be corrected, but mistakes made during this stage become extremely difficult to correct later on in life. This stage is defined by the child developing a close, or best, friend. If a child does

not learn intimacy in this stage, they face difficulties with sexual partners later on in life.

- **Early Adolescence (thirteen–seventeen years):** This epoch starts with the beginning of puberty. The need for friendship now exists alongside a need for sexual expression as interest begins to focus on the opposite sex. During this stage, the lust dynamism first appears. If a child does not have a capacity for intimacy already in place, love and lust might be confused with one another and the individual may have sexual relationships that feature no real intimacy.
- **Late Adolescence (eighteen–twenty-three years):** While this epoch can occur when an individual is as young as sixteen years old, late adolescence sets in once an individual has the ability to experience both intimacy and lust toward one person, and a long-term relationship is the main focus of the

individual. This epoch is also characterized by the individual learning how to cope with life in the adult world.

- **Adulthood (twenty-three years and older):** During this epoch, the individual establishes his or her career, financial security, and family, and his or her pattern for viewing the world is stable. If there is success in the earlier epochs, relationships and socialization become far easier; however, if success does not occur in previous epochs, interpersonal conflicts that lead to anxiety will be much more common.

From Harry Stack Sullivan's extensive work in personality came interpersonal psychoanalysis, a form of psychoanalysis that focused on understanding the present psychopathy of an individual by looking at the interactions of his or her past. While Sullivan's theories have become less popular, his influence in psychology remains.

THE MAGICAL NUMBER SEVEN, PLUS OR MINUS TWO

Memory limits

In 1956, cognitive psychologist George A. Miller published his now-famous paper entitled "The Magical Number Seven, Plus or Minus Two: Some Limits on Our Capacity for Processing Information." In it, Miller theorized that a person's short-term memory (STM) can only hold around seven items, plus or minus two, at any given time. In order to deal with any information that is larger than seven items, we must first organize this information into large chunks. For example, by combining words into sentences, or combining sentences into stories, we are able to hold more than seven words in our short-term memory. However, our memory still only has the ability to hold seven of these chunks at one time. For example, an individual will have a hard time being able to recall a sequence such as this because there are more than seven numbers:

4 8 1 9 7 6 2 0 1 3

However, by naturally grouping these numbers into chunks, our short-term memory will be able to recall these numbers. In the sequence above, if we group the numbers together (let's say we group them as something familiar, like years), we can then make that sequence of ten numbers into the following sequence:

4 – 8 – 1976 – 2013

Before, we would have struggled to recall ten individual numbers, but now we only have a string consisting of four chunks, and it is much easier to remember.

In order to improve the capacity of one's short-term memory, the information must be organized into bigger chunks. By taking little parts and organizing them into larger wholes, one has the ability to improve his or her memory.

RECODING

In Miller's paper, he cited the work of psychologist Sydney Smith, who was able to memorize long arrangements of four binary digits—numbers composed of 1s and 0s. The arrangements of binary numbers are the equivalent of a single decimal digit. For example, the number 2 is expressed as 0 0 1 0. Smith realized that sixteen binary numbers could be expressed as four decimal numbers, and used this 4:1 ratio to increase his memory span from being able to remember ten binary digits to being able to remember forty binary digits. By the end of his work, Smith was able to memorize ten consecutive decimal numbers and convert them to binary digits, creating a list of forty binary numbers.

In 1980, psychologists K. Anders Ericsson, Herbert Simon, and Bill Chase decided to expand upon this notion of recoding. For an hour a day, three to five days a week, and for more than a year and a half, the psychologists had an undergraduate student memorize strings of random decimal digits. Incredibly, by the end of the study, the student's memory span went from being able to remember seven digits, to being able to remember seventy-nine digits. Immediately after hearing a string of seventy-nine random digits, the student was able to flawlessly repeat the series of digits back, and could even recall sequences of digits from previous days.

The student involved in the study was not given any particular method to code these numbers, and instead applied his own personal experience to the process. Being a runner, he recoded these number sequences as running times—the number 3593 became 3 minutes and 59 point 3 seconds. Later on, he used age as a method for coding.

The work of George A. Miller and Ericsson, Simon, and Chase shows that when intricate and elaborate coding schemes are used to create organization, a person's memory will actually work better.

ERICH FROMM (1900–1980)

Fundamental human needs

Erich Fromm, the only child of Orthodox Jewish parents, was born in Frankfurt, Germany, on March 23rd, 1900. Fromm described his childhood as being orthodox and incredibly neurotic, and his religious upbringing would have a great impact on his work in psychology.

During the beginning of World War I, Fromm took an interest in understanding group behavior, and at just fourteen years old, he began studying the work of Sigmund Freud and Karl Marx. In 1922, Fromm graduated from the University of Heidelberg with a PhD in sociology and began working as a psychoanalyst. As the Nazi party came to power, Fromm fled Germany and began teaching at Columbia University in New York City, where he would meet and work with Karen Horney and Abraham Maslow.

Fromm is considered to be one of the most important figures in psychoanalysis during the twentieth century and had a great influence on humanistic psychology. Like Carl Jung, Alfred Adler, Karen Horney, and Erik Erikson, Fromm belonged to a group known as the Neo-Freudians. The group agreed with much of what Freud claimed, but were also very critical of particular parts and incorporated their own beliefs into Freud's theories.

Fromm's work combined the ideas of Sigmund Freud and Karl Marx. While Freud placed emphasis on the unconscious and biology, Marx emphasized the role of society and economic systems. Fromm believed that there were times when biological factors played a large role in determining the outcome of an individual, and there were other times when social factors played a large role. However, Fromm then introduced what he believed was the true nature of humanity: freedom. Fromm is most known for his work in political psychology, human character, and love. In 1944, Fromm moved to Mexico, where he would eventually create the Mexican Institute of Psychoanalysis and work as director until 1976. On March 18th, 1980, Erich Fromm died from a heart attack in Muralto, Switzerland.

The Neo-Freudian Disagreements

While the Neo-Freudians developed their own theories, they shared similar problems with Freud's work. These included:

- Freud's negative view of humanity
- Freud's belief that an individual's personality is mostly, if not entirely, shaped by his or her childhood experiences
- Freud's failure to include the impact that social and cultural influences can have on personality and behavior

Fromm stated that freedom—not to be confused with liberty or political freedom—is something that people actively try to flee from. But why would someone try to avoid being free? While Fromm agreed with the common belief that in order for there to be individual freedom, there must be freedom from external authority, he also claimed that there are psychological processes within people that limit and restrain freedom. Therefore, in order for an individual to achieve a true form of freedom, he or she must first overcome these psychological processes.

According to Fromm, freedom means being independent and relying on no one but your own self for any sense of purpose or meaning. This can lead to feelings of isolation, fear, alienation, and insignificance. In severe cases, the truest form of freedom could even lead to mental illness. Fromm eventually concluded that because freedom is psychologically difficult to have, people will try to avoid it. He postulated three main ways that this can happen:

1. **Authoritarianism:** People will join and become part of an authoritarian society by submitting their power or becoming the authority. While Fromm noted that extreme versions of this were sadism and masochism, less extreme types of authoritarianism can be seen everywhere, such as with the teacher and student.
2. **Destructiveness:** This is when people will destroy anything around them in response to their own suffering. It is from destructiveness that humiliation, brutality, and crimes are created. Destructiveness can also be directed inward; this is known as self-destructiveness and the most obvious example is suicide. While Freud believed that destructiveness was the result of self-destructiveness being directed onto others, Fromm believed the opposite to be true, claiming that self-destructiveness was the result

of being frustrated with destructiveness.

3. **Automaton conformity:** In societies that are less hierarchical, people have the ability to hide in mass culture. By disappearing into the crowd—be it how one talks, dresses, thinks, etc.—a person no longer has to take responsibility, and therefore does not have to acknowledge his or her freedom.

The choices that people make in how they will avoid their freedom can depend on the type of family they grew up in. According to Fromm, a family that is healthy and productive is one where parents are responsible for providing their children an atmosphere of love when teaching about reasoning. This will enable the children to grow up learning how to take responsibility and acknowledge their freedom. However, unproductive families also exist, and these are families, Fromm reasoned, that promote avoidance behavior:

1. **Symbiotic families:** In this type of family, the personalities of members do not fully develop because other members of the family “swallow them up.” For example, when a child’s personality simply reflects his or her parents’ wishes, or when a child is so controlling over his or her parents that the parents’ existence revolves around serving their child.
2. **Withdrawing families:** In this type of family, parents expect their children to live up to very high standards and are incredibly demanding of their children. This type of parenting also involves ritualized punishment, usually paired with the children being told that this is done “for their own good.” Another form of punishment found in this type of family is not physical but rather emotional, with the use of guilt or removal of any type of affection.

Fromm believed that parenting was only one part of the equation, however. He claimed that people are so used to following orders that they act out these orders without even realizing they are doing it, and that the rules of society are embedded into our unconscious and hold people back from truly attaining freedom. He called this the social unconscious.

FROMM'S HUMAN NEEDS

Fromm distinguished between "human needs" and "animal needs." Animal needs, according to Fromm, are the basic physiological needs, while human needs are what help people find the answer to their existence and signify a desire to reunite with the natural world.

In Fromm's conception, there are eight human needs:

1. **Relatedness:** The need for relationships with other people.
2. **Transcendence:** Because people are put into this world without their consent, we have the

need to surpass, or transcend, our nature by creating or destroying.

3. **Rootedness:** The need to create roots and feel at home in this world. If done productively, this will result in growing past the ties between mother and child; however, if not carried out productively, this can result in being afraid to move past the security of one's mother.
4. **A sense of identity:** Fromm believed in order for one to remain sane, a person needs to have a sense of individuality. This desire for an identity can be so intense that it can cause a person to conform, which will not create an individual identity but rather will make someone take and develop an identity from others.
5. **A frame of orientation:** A person needs to understand the world and how he or she fits into it. People can find structure in their religion, science, their personal philosophies, or anything that

helps provide them a reference angle from which to view the world.

6. **Excitation and stimulation:** Actively trying to accomplish a goal instead of just responding.
7. **Unity:** The need to feel united with the natural world and the human world.
8. **Effectiveness:** The need to feel as though you are accomplished.

Erich Fromm is considered to be one of the most important and influential psychologists of the twentieth century. He played a key role in humanistic psychology, and viewed humanity as a contradiction. Life, according to Fromm, was a desire to be both a part of nature and separate from nature, and freedom was actually something that people actively try to avoid.

THE GOOD SAMARITAN EXPERIMENT

Understanding help

In 1978, psychologists John Darley and Daniel Batson created an experiment based on the old parable of the Good Samaritan found in the Bible.

The Good Samaritan Parable

In this parable, a Jewish man traveling from Jerusalem to Jericho is robbed, beaten, and left on the road to die. As he lies there, a Rabbi walks by him and instead of helping the man, as he should, the Rabbi pretends not to see the man, and walks to the other side of the road. Then, a Levite walks near the man. However, instead of helping the poor man, the Levite simply looks at him and then walks to the other side of the road, like the Rabbi had done before. Then a Samaritan walks near the injured man on the road. Even though the Samaritans and the Jewish people are enemies, the Samaritan binds the man's wounds, takes him to an inn, and cares for him that night. The next morning, the Samaritan pays the innkeeper and tells him to take care of the gentleman, saying that he will pay for however much it costs.

Darley and Batson set out to test three hypotheses:

1. It has been said that the Rabbi and Levite did not help the man because their minds were focused on religious matters, and they were therefore too distracted. The first hypothesis to be tested by Darley and Batson was to see if people who think about religion are less persuaded to help than a person who is not primarily focused on religion.
2. The second hypothesis was whether people who are in a hurry

are less likely to help or express helping behavior.

3. The third hypothesis was whether people who turn to religion to understand the meaning of life and gain spiritual insights are more likely to help than a person who turns to religion for personal gain.

EXPERMIENT

THE GOOD SAMARITAN EXPERIMENT

The test subjects of this experiment are religious studies students, who first must complete a questionnaire regarding their religious affiliation and what they believe in, which is used to evaluate the third hypothesis.

1. The students are first taught a class lecture on religious studies, and then they are told that they have to travel to another building.
2. Between the buildings, an actor lies on the ground appearing injured and in dire need of help.
3. To test how a sense of urgency affects the subjects, some students

are told to rush, that they have only a few moments to reach the other building. The other students are told that there is no need to hurry.

4. To test the mindset of the subjects, some students are instructed that they will be giving a talk on the parable of the Good Samaritan once they reach their destination, while others are instructed that they will have to lecture about seminary procedures.
5. To assess the behavior of the subjects, a six-point plan is created that ranges from not even noticing the injured man to remaining with him until help arrives.

THE RESULTS

In their experiment, Darley and Batson found that the haste of the subject was the main determining factor in whether or not they stopped to help the injured man. When the subjects were not in any type of hurry, 63 percent of the subjects stopped to help the injured man. However, if the subjects were in a rush, only 10 percent of the subjects stopped to help the man.

Those who were ordered to give a speech about the Good Samaritan were almost twice as likely to stop and help the man as those who were ordered to lecture about seminary procedures. This shows that the thoughts of an individual do play a factor in whether or not a person will help. However, this factor is not as impactful as whether or not the person is in a hurry, because the majority of those in a hurry that were lecturing about the Good Samaritan did not provide assistance to the man.

Lastly, whether an individual was religious for personal gain or for spiritual insight did not seem to matter.

When students reached their destination, some who had ignored the injured man began to express feelings of anxiousness and guilt, which seemingly indicated that not helping the injured man was due to feelings of time constraints and pressure, not because of an overall uncaring attitude.

In the case of the Good Samaritan experiment, the researchers were able to successfully show that an individual’s failure to stop and help a “victim” was solely based on his or her preoccupation with time, and that being so wrapped up in one’s head can have startling results.

PERSONALITY DISORDERS

When behavior goes astray

Personality disorders are patterns of behavior and inner experiences that stray from the norms of the culture that a person belongs to. These patterns are inflexible and inescapable, begin in adolescence or as a young adult, and can cause serious distress or damage in a person's daily life.

Researchers are still unsure what causes personality disorders. While some believe these disorders are the result of genetics, others believe the root of personality disorders can be found in early life experiences that prevent normal behavior and thought patterns from developing.

DIAGNOSING A PERSONALITY DISORDER

Psychologists diagnose personality disorders based on criteria established in the Diagnostic and Statistical Manual of Mental Disorders (DSM-IV). Symptoms an individual must exhibit are:

- The patterns of behavior must affect different parts of the person's life, including, but not limited to, relationships, work, and social life.
- The patterns of behavior must be long-lasting and prevalent.
- The symptoms must affect two or more of the following: feelings, thoughts, the ability to control impulses, and functioning with other people.
- The pattern of behavior must begin in adolescence or as a young adult.
- The pattern of behavior must be unchanging over time.
- These symptoms cannot be the result of other medical conditions or mental illnesses, or drug abuse.

THE DIFFERENT TYPES OF PERSONALITY DISORDERS

There are ten different types of personality disorders, and these can be categorized into three distinct clusters based on similar characteristics.

Cluster A

Personality disorders in this cluster are represented by eccentric and odd behavior. These include:

1. **Paranoid Personality Disorder:** This personality disorder is characterized by symptoms resembling schizophrenia, and is seen in 2 percent of the adult population in the United States. The symptoms include constant suspicion and distrust of other people; feeling as if one is being exploited, deceived, or lied to; trying to find hidden meanings in things like conversations and hand gestures; feeling like partners, family, and friends are untrustworthy and disloyal; and having outbursts of anger as a result of feeling deceived. People who suffer from

paranoid personality disorder often seem serious, jealous, secretive, and cold.

2. **Schizoid Personality Disorder:** This is a somewhat rare type of personality disorder; it is therefore unknown what percentage of the population is affected by this disorder, but it is understood that men are affected more than women. Symptoms of schizoid personality disorder include little to no desire to have any close relationships with other people, rarely participating in fun or pleasurable activities, being detached from others, and being indifferent to rejection, criticism, affirmation, or praise. People that suffer from schizoid personality disorder usually seem withdrawn, indifferent, and cold.
3. **Schizotypal Personality Disorder:** This type of personality disorder affects around 3 percent of the adult population in the United States. Symptoms of

schizotypal personality disorder include: having eccentric views, behavior, and thoughts, facing difficulties when it comes to having relationships, having a severe form of social anxiety that does not go away regardless of circumstances, a belief in one's ability to read minds, or see into the future, having inappropriate reactions, ignoring other people, and talking to oneself. People suffering from schizotypal personality disorder are more at risk of developing psychotic disorders and depression.

Cluster B

Personality disorders in this cluster are characterized by behavior that is erratic and dramatic. These include:

1. **Antisocial Personality Disorder:** This type of personality disorder is found more often in men (3 percent) than women (1 percent). Symptoms of antisocial personality disorder include having

a complete disregard for the safety of other people and oneself, being deceitful, being impulsive, being very aggressive and irritable (and as a result, constantly getting into fights), being apathetic towards others, and failing to conform to the norms that have been established by society. As a result, people with antisocial personality disorder are often in trouble with the law.

2. **Borderline Personality Disorder:** This type of personality disorder affects around 1–2 percent of the adult population in the United States, and is found more often in men than women. Symptoms of borderline personality disorder include suffering from intense bouts of depression, anxiety, and irritability—ranging anywhere from a few hours to a few days—impulsiveness, participating in self-destructive behavior like drug abuse or eating disorders as a

means to manipulate others, and experiencing a prevalent pattern of interpersonal relationships that are unstable and intense as a result of having a low self-image, a poor self-identity, and constantly idealizing and undervaluing the other person in the relationship.

3. **Histrionic Personality Disorder:** This type of personality disorder is found more often in women than men, and affects 2–3 percent of the adult population of the United States. Symptoms of histrionic personality disorder include a constant need to be the center of attention, exhibiting inappropriate behavior that is sexual or provocative in nature, expressing shallow emotions that constantly change, being easily influenced by other people, thinking of relationships as being much more intimate than they really are, and speaking in a way that lacks any real detail and is overdramatic and theatrical.

4. **Narcissistic Personality Disorder:** This type of personality disorder is found in less than 1 percent of the adult population in the United States. Symptoms of narcissistic personality disorder include having a grandiose idea of one's own self-importance, being preoccupied with fantasies of power and success, holding a belief that the narcissist is unique and should only associate with—and can only be understood by—those people that are of the same status, feeling entitled and deserving of special treatment, being jealous of other people, believing that other people are jealous of them, taking advantage of others for personal gain, being apathetic towards others, and constantly desiring praise, affirmation, and attention.

Cluster C

Personality disorders in this cluster are characterized by feelings and behavior based on fear and anxiety.

1. **Avoidant Personality Disorder:** This type of personality disorder affects around 1 percent of the adult population in the United States, and those who suffer from it are at risk of also developing anxiety disorders such as social phobia and agoraphobia. Symptoms of avoidant personality disorder include feeling inadequate, being incredibly shy, being very sensitive when it comes to any type of rejection or criticism, avoiding social and interpersonal interactions (like work or school), having low self-esteem, and wishing to be close with other people but having trouble creating relationships with anyone that is not part of the individual's immediate family.
2. **Dependent Personality Disorder:** This type of personality disorder can be found in around 2.5 percent of the adult population in the United States. Those who suffer from this will usually also be

suffering from borderline, avoidant, or histrionic personality disorders. Symptoms of dependent personality disorder include being sensitive to any type of rejection or criticism, having low self-confidence and self-esteem, concentrating on abandonment, taking a passive role in a relationship, experiencing trouble making decisions on their own, and avoiding any sort of responsibility.

3. **Obsessive-Compulsive Personality Disorder:** This type of personality disorder affects approximately 1 percent of the adult population in the United States, and occurs in males twice as often as it does in females. Individuals who suffer from this disorder are also at risk of developing medical illnesses caused by stress and anxiety disorders. Symptoms of obsessive-compulsive personality disorder include feeling helpless in any situation that the individual cannot

completely control, being preoccupied with order, control, rules, lists, and perfection, being unable to throw away items even though they have no sentimental value to the person, striving for perfection to the point where it actually hinders an individual from completing his or her goal, being devoted to work so much so that all other items are excluded, and being inflexible and resistant when it comes to change. People who suffer from this disorder are often viewed as stubborn and rigid, and are often miserly, viewing money solely as something to be saved for an oncoming disaster and not something to be spent on themselves or others. It should be noted that though obsessive-compulsive personality disorder (OCPD) shares many similarities with obsessive-compulsive anxiety disorder (OCD), the two are considered completely separate disorders.

Because personality is so crucial to experience, when an individual behaves and interacts during everyday life in ways that stray from the norms set forth by his or her culture, it can have a truly dramatic effect on that person. By understanding personality disorders and breaking them down into distinct categories, psychologists are able to further understand and help treat people suffering from these conditions.

DISSOCIATIVE DISORDERS

Don't pardon the interruption

Dissociative disorders are disorders that occur as a result of a disturbance, interruption, or dissociation with an individual's perception, memory, identity, or consciousness. When these fundamental aspects don't work properly, the result places the individual under a large amount of psychological distress. While there are several types of dissociative disorders, they all share certain characteristics.

Psychologists believe these types of disorders all stem from the individual experiencing some type of trauma in his or her lifetime. The individual then uses dissociation as a type of coping mechanism, because the situation or experience is simply too difficult and traumatic for it to be incorporated into the conscious self. Oftentimes, dissociative disorders, or symptoms of dissociative disorders, are found in other specific mental illnesses, including panic disorder, obsessive-compulsive disorder, and posttraumatic stress disorder.

There are four types of dissociative disorders:

1. **Dissociative amnesia:** In this type of dissociative disorder, an individual blocks critical information that usually pertains to a stressful or traumatic event. Dissociative amnesia can be further broken down into four types:

    - **Localized amnesia:** When any memories relating to a specific, usually traumatic, event are completely absent. Localized amnesia is time-sensitive. For example, if an individual had a car accident and cannot recall any memories from the accident until three days later, then he or she is experiencing this type of dissociative amnesia.
    - **Selective amnesia:** When an individual can remember bits and pieces of an event that occurred within

a specific period of time. For example, if a person has been physically abused and he or she can only remember certain parts of what occurred around the time of the abuse.

- **Generalized amnesia:** When a person cannot remember a single detail about his or her life. This type of dissociative amnesia is very rare.
- **Systematized amnesia:** When the person's amnesia only affects a particular category of information. For example, a person may not be able to remember anything that relates to one specific location or person.

If a patient suffers from selective, generalized, or systematized amnesia, there is often a larger, more complex type of dissociative disorder that is responsible, like dissociative identity disorder.

2. **Dissociative fugue:** This is a very rare dissociative disorder where a person suddenly, and without any planning, leaves his or her environment

and travels far from his or her home. These trips can last anywhere from hours to months. There have been cases of people who suffer from dissociative fugue that have traveled thousands of miles. While in the fugue state, people will show signs of amnesia, having no understanding of why they left in the first place and struggling with remembering their past. The individual will be confused about, or have zero recollection of, his or her identity; and in some rare cases, people have even taken on new identities.

3. **Dissociative identity disorder:** At one time referred to as multiple personality disorder, this is the most well-known example of a dissociative disorder. In dissociative identity disorder, an individual has many distinct personalities and identities, rather than just the one. At the very least, two of the individual's personalities must show up repeatedly and take control of the individual's behavior to qualify as having

dissociative identity disorder. Fifty percent of all people suffering from this disorder have less than eleven identities, though there are cases where an individual has as many as 100 identities.

The dissociative personalities all have their own unique identity, self-image, history, and name. When a person becomes one of these other identities—known as alters—the individual experiences long gaps in his or her memory. It can take seconds for an individual to shift to one of his or her alters, and these alters can have different ages, nationalities, genders, sexual preferences, and even different body languages and postures than the individual. The appearance and departure of the personalities are commonly triggered by a stressful event.

People who suffer from dissociative identity disorder will often have other disorders, such as borderline personality disorder, depression, eating disorders, and substance abuse. This combination can frequently result in violence, self-mutilation, and suicidal tendencies.

4. **Depersonalization disorder:** A person suffering from depersonalization disorder experiences feelings of detachment. The individual's body feels unreal to him or her. While symptoms of depersonalization are different for everybody, the most common descriptions of this experience are feeling like one's body is dissolving or changing, feeling like the individual is actually watching his or her life unfold as an external observer, feeling like the individual is floating on the ceiling while looking down at him or herself, and feeling like he or she is some sort of robot or machine. Most people who suffer from depersonalization disorder also experience emotional detachment and feel emotionally numb.

Just because a person experiences depersonalization does not necessarily mean they suffer from depersonalization disorder. Depersonalization is often a symptom for other conditions, such as panic disorders, acute stress disorder, posttraumatic stress disorder, and borderline personality disorder. If depersonalization only occurs when the individual experiences a traumatic stressor or panic attack, then they do not have depersonalization disorder.

Depersonalization can also occur in perfectly normal people. Sleep deprivation, emotionally stressful events, use of particular anesthetics, and experimental conditions such as those involving weightlessness can all create the effect of depersonalization.

Because depersonalization is such a common occurrence, it is only when these symptoms become so severe that a large amount of emotional distress is placed on the individual and there is an interference with functioning at a normal level that depersonalization disorder is diagnosed.

THE ROSENHAN EXPERIMENT

What happens when you place the sane in the insane?

In 1973, Stanford University professor David Rosenhan questioned the entire notion of psychiatric diagnosis by creating an experiment to test whether psychiatrists could tell the difference between a sane person and an insane person in any sort of reliable way. If they could not, according to Rosenhan, psychiatrists could not reliably diagnose an abnormality in any meaningful way. Rosenhan's experiment was made up of two parts:

THE EXPERIMENT WITH PSEUDOPATIENTS

For the experiment, Rosenhan recruited eight individuals. There were three psychologists, a psychiatrist, a pediatrician, a housewife, a painter, and a graduate student studying psychology. In total, there were five men and three women.

His first goal was to have these people gain admission into twelve different hospitals across five different states. In order to have results be as generalized as possible, the hospitals ranged from new to old, research-based to not research-based, poorly staffed to well staffed, and they were funded privately, federally, and through a university. Rosenhan had these eight people, whom he referred to as "pseudopatients," make an appointment with hospitals. Once they were brought into the admissions offices, they would all complain about hearing unfamiliar voices in their heads that were of the same sex.

After the pseudopatients were successfully admitted into the psychiatric hospitals, they stopped pretending to have any abnormal symptoms. They spoke with the staff and patients of the hospital the way they would speak to any other person in their daily life; and when asked how they were feeling, they would tell the staff they felt fine and were not experiencing any symptoms. The pseudopatients were told that it was up to them to convince the hospital staff to release them and make them believe that they were sane (without making mention of the experiment). While inside of the hospital, the pseudopatients made notes of their experiences and observations. To compare his results, Rosenhan had a student ask a series of questions to staff at Stanford's health center. The answers to these questions (given when the staff was aware they were on the record with their answers) were then compared to the answers the pseudopatients were told when they asked staff members questions.

THE PSEUDOPATIENT RESULTS

The average hospital stay for the patients was nineteen days, with some staying for only seven days and others staying for as long as fifty-two days. Every patient except one was admitted into the hospitals with a diagnosis of schizophrenia, and when they left, they were diagnosed with "schizophrenia in remission." These diagnoses were given even though none of the patients exhibited a clear symptom of schizophrenia.

While other patients in the hospital raised suspicions about the pseudopatients and claimed that they were journalists placed in there to check up on the hospital, the hospital staff actually viewed the normal behavior of the pseudopatients as part of their illnesses. Records from the nurses of three separate pseudopatients claimed that the act of writing they were engaging in was a pathological behavior. Rosenhan concluded that there are similarities between the insane and sane, such as moods and emotions; however, when placed into the world of a psychiatric hospital, it was commonly found that experiences and moods that people encounter every day and are usually seen as normal, are instead seen as pathological.

None of the participants involved in the study enjoyed their stays at the mental institutions, and stated that the facilities deprived patients of many human rights and left individuals with feelings of powerlessness and depersonalization. Patients were not allowed to move around as they pleased; many toilets were missing doors; and staff members were cruel to patients.

Of the estimated 2,100 medication tablets that were given to the pseudopatients, only two were ever swallowed. Most were simply flushed down the toilet, where the pseudopatients found medication from other patients. Rosenhan concluded that as long as the actions of patients were viewed as cooperative, no one noticed their behavior.

A SECONDARY STUDY

Following the first part of his study, Rosenhan visited a research hospital that had been aware of his initial research with the pseudopatients. He proceeded to lie to the staff, telling them that over the next three months, other pseudopatients would try to gain entry into their hospital. The hospital staff was told to rate all new patients on a 10-point scale as to the likelihood that they were one of the pseudopatients.

Over that time period, there were a total of 193 (real) patients judged. Forty-one patients were believed to be pseudopatients according to one staff member; twenty-three patients were believed to be the pseudopatients according to a psychiatrist; and nineteen patients were believed to be the pseudopatients according to one staff member and a psychiatrist.

According to Rosenhan, this second study demonstrated that psychiatrists are unable to reliably differentiate between a sane person and an insane person. While the first part of his study showed failure in being able to identify sanity, the second part of his study showed failure in being able to identify insanity. Rosenhan illustrated that with psychiatric labels in particular, anything that a patient does is then interpreted in relation to this psychiatric label. Instead, Rosenhan suggests that rather than labeling an individual as insane, hospital workers and psychiatrists should pay attention to the behavior and specific problems of the individual.

EVALUATION OF THE ROSENHAN EXPERIMENT

While Rosenhan's experiment showed the limitations of classifying patients and revealed the awful conditions of mental hospitals at that time, because his study was based entirely on lying to the hospital staff, it is considered unethical. Rosenhan's work did, however, change the philosophy that many institutions took when it came to how to approach mental care.

At the time of Rosenhan's study, the Diagnostic and Statistical Manual of Mental Disorders that was being used for diagnosing was DSM-II. In the 1980s, DSM-III was introduced with the purpose of addressing problems of unclear criteria and unreliability. Many have argued that with DSM-III, Rosenhan would not have the same results. The current model being used today is DSM-IV.

DAVID KOLB'S LEARNING STYLES

Learning by experience

In 1984, philosophy professor David Kolb developed a new model of learning styles and a theory of learning. Kolb's learning theory can be broken down into two parts: a cycle of learning that is made up of four distinct stages, and four distinct styles of learning.

Kolb defined learning as when abstract concepts are acquired and have the ability to be applied within an array of situations, and when new experiences motivate new concepts to arise.

KOLB'S FOUR-STAGE LEARNING CYCLE

In Kolb's theory of learning, there are four stages of a "learning cycle." When a person is learning, they go through all four stages.

1. **Concrete Experience:** A person faces a new experience or reinterprets an experience that has previously existed.
2. **Reflective Observation:** This is the observation of any new experience. Inconsistencies between understanding and the experience are particularly noteworthy.
3. **Abstract Conceptualization:** From reflection comes a new idea. This can also pertain to the modification of an abstract concept that already exists.
4. **Active Experimentation:** The individual then applies this idea to the world and sees what the end results are.

KOLB'S EXPERIENTIAL LEARNING STYLES

From these four stages, Kolb maps out four distinct learning styles. According to Kolb, different people prefer different learning styles, and this is influenced by numerous factors, including the educational experiences, cognitive structure, and social environment of the individual. No matter what the influences are, an individual's preference in learning style is the product of two choices. Kolb expressed these choices, or variables, as an axis. On opposite ends of the lines are conflicting modes: Feeling (Concrete Experience, or CE) vs. Thinking (Abstract Conceptualization, or AC), and Doing (Abstract Experimentation, or AE) vs. Watching (Reflective Observation, or RO).

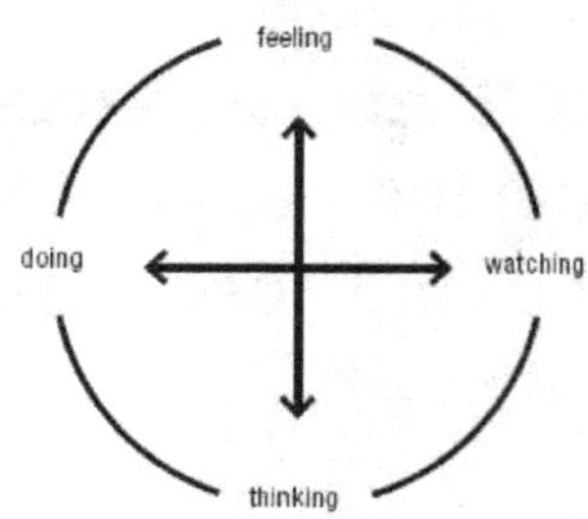

INTERSECTING AXES OF LEARNING STYLES

The east-west axis is known as the "processing continuum," and it deals with how a person approaches a given task. The north-south axis is referred to as the "perception continuum," and it deals with the emotional response of an individual. According to Kolb, an individual cannot experience the two variables on a single axis at once.

With this information, Kolb then identified four learning styles that people use depending on where they fall on the continuum: accommodating, diverging, converging, and assimilating. While every person uses the different types of learning styles, some are preferred more than others. To better understand how these learning styles work, consider the following diagram and chart:

	ACTIVE EXPERIMENTATION (AE)	REFLECTIVE OBSERVATION (RO)
Concrete Experience (CE)	Accommodating (CE/AE)	Diverging (CE/RO)
Abstract Conceptualization (AC)	Converging (AC/AE)	Assimilating (AC/RO)

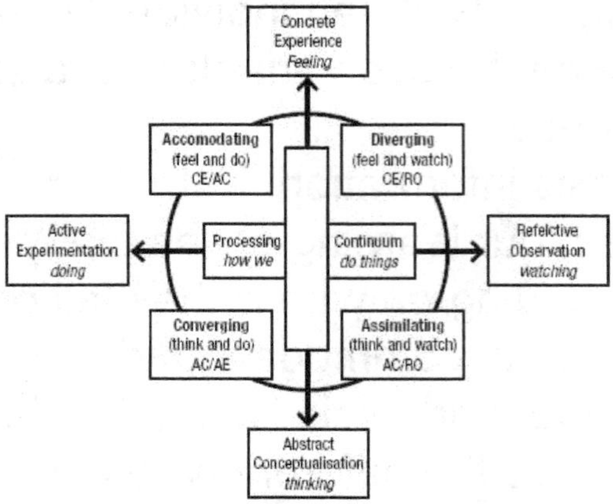

MORE DETAILED LOOK AT KOLB'S THEORY

Accommodating (CE/AE): Doing and Feeling

This type of learning style depends on the use of intuition instead of logic. Often, people employing it will follow their "gut instinct." When a person has an accommodating learning style, he or she will commonly depend on other people for information and then analyze this information on his or her own. These types of people enjoy seeing plans through, and are attracted to new situations and challenges.

Diverging (CE/RO): Feeling and Watching

People that have a diverging learning style prefer watching instead of doing, and solve problems through gathering information and using their imagination. Because of this, individuals with diverging learning styles have the ability to look at situations from different viewpoints, and are most adept when placed in situations where the generation of ideas is needed. Individuals with diverging learning styles tend to also be sensitive, emotional, and more artistic, and they tend to enjoy working with others, getting feedback, gaining information, and listening to what others have to say with an open mind.

Converging (AC/AE): Doing and Thinking

Individuals that have converging learning styles are more technically oriented, and prefer to solve problems to practical issues instead of interpersonal issues. People that have this type of learning style are most adept when solving practical problems and making decisions by finding answers to questions. As a result, people with a converging learning style enjoy experimenting, simulating, and working with real-world applications.

Assimilating (AC/RO): Watching and Thinking

In assimilating learning styles, emphasis is placed on taking a logical approach to abstract ideas and concepts, and there is less focus placed on people or practical applications. Individuals with a preference for an assimilating learning style can understand a wide range of information and have the ability to assemble the information into a logical format. For this reason, an assimilating learning style works best in a scientific field. People that have assimilating learning styles also prefer being able to think through a situation and examine analytical models.

Having a firm understanding of one's own learning style and the learning styles of others can be extremely important and have very real-world applications. Individuals can understand how to communicate information to others in a way that will be the most effective, and understand what they themselves need to improve upon.

ANXIETY DISORDERS

More than just nerves

While anxiety and stress are emotions experienced by everyone, anxiety disorders are serious forms of mental illness that cause great distress and take on a crippling effect, preventing a person from being able to live a normal and healthy life. There are six different types of anxiety disorders. They are:

PANIC DISORDER

When an individual suffers from panic disorder, they will experience intense panic attacks, which are often triggered without any reason or warning. The symptoms of a panic attack include:

- Sweating excessively
- Having chest pain
- Shaking
- Being short of breath or feeling as if you are choking

- Having hot or cold flashes
- Having heart palpitations
- Feeling dizzy, lightheaded, or having vertigo
- Experiencing a tingling or numbing sensation
- Having stomach cramps or experiencing any other type of digestive discomfort such as nausea
- Having a very overwhelming fear of death and losing control

These panic attacks will usually hit their peak at some point within the first ten minutes, though they are capable of lasting longer, and many sufferers will still feel anxious hours after the panic attack has ended.

The Relationship Between Agoraphobia and Panic Disorder

There is a common misconception that agoraphobia is a fear of open spaces. This is incorrect. Agoraphobia is actually when an individual fears that he or she might have a panic attack when he or she is in a location or situation (such as open spaces), and that this panic attack will make the individual incredibly embarrassed. The person becomes so fixated on when the next panic attack might occur that he or she no longer wishes to go to these places or participate in these activities. Agoraphobia usually occurs as a result of panic disorder, though there are cases where an individual suffers from agoraphobia without having panic disorder. Around one-third of the people who suffer from panic disorder also suffer from agoraphobia.

OBSESSIVE-COMPULSIVE DISORDER

This is the most active type of anxiety disorder. The anxiety from this disorder comes from the individual having constant obsessions, which are distressing thoughts and ideas that are not wanted and will not go away. The person tries to relieve this stress by performing ritualistic behaviors. Eventually, however, these rituals turn into compulsions, and the individual continues to repeat this behavior. The compulsions can be so complex that they can greatly disrupt any sort of daily routine. Most of the time the compulsions are linked to the obsessions themselves, like people repeatedly washing their hands every ten minutes because they think their hands are contaminated, but this does not apply to all compulsions.

People who suffer from obsessive-compulsive disorder are usually aware of how irrational their behavior is, and it often becomes a source of regular frustration and confusion for them. While obsessive-compulsive disorder can occur at any age, symptoms usually appear within two distinct periods: before puberty, which is referred to as early-onset OCD, and later in life, which is known as late-onset OCD. There are five different types of obsessive-compulsive disorder:

1. **Obsessions with contamination and compulsions of cleaning or washing:** When a person focuses on feeling dirty and the discomfort associated with not being clean. To reduce these feelings, a person will wash his or her hands excessively, sometimes for hours.
2. **Obsessions of being harmed or harming others and compulsions of checking:** An example of this type of obsession might be someone who believes (obsessively) that his or her house will burn down. As a result, people constantly have to check the oven, toaster, and stove, continually check that the light switches are turned off, and even constantly drive to their house to make sure it is not burning down.
3. **Pure obsessions:** These are obsessions that don't seem to have any visual compulsions. Instead, these obsessions revolve around things of religious, sexual,

and aggressive nature. For example, an individual constantly having the obsession that he or she is a murderer and will kill someone. To relieve stress, mental rituals are often used, where an individual will count in his or her head, pray, or recite certain words.

4. **Obsessions of symmetry and compulsions of counting, ordering, and arranging:** People that experience this type of OCD have a strong urge to order and arrange objects until they believe they have done so perfectly. People with this type of OCD may also experience the urge to repeat words or sentences until a certain task is executed perfectly. In some cases, this compulsion is performed with the idea that if it is performed correctly, they will be able to ward off possible dangers. For example, when a woman rearranges her desk in a particular way with the mentality that if she does this, her

husband won't get into a car accident.

5. **Hoarding:** The act of collecting objects that usually have little to no actual value, and never throwing them away. This can result in clutter so severe that people sometimes have trouble living in their own homes because of the sheer mass of what has been collected. Usually when people hoard, they have the obsession that the things they are saving will be able to be used one day. An individual can also have compulsive hoarding without having obsessive-compulsive disorder.

POSTTRAUMATIC STRESS DISORDER

This type of anxiety disorder occurs after an individual has been exposed to or has experienced a traumatic event where they felt that they, or those around them, were in danger of being hurt or killed.

Once a traumatic event has occurred, an individual will begin having flashbacks, distressing dreams, and intrusive images and thoughts relating back to the trauma. Individuals will also avoid any situations that might remind them of the event, since when they are exposed to any cues that remind them of the trauma, they will experience great emotional distress. In addition to this, the individual's behavior will change, and he or she will limit the activities he or she participates in, have difficulty expressing a full spectrum of emotions, and may seem to lose hope for his or her future.

SOCIAL ANXIETY DISORDER

This is one of the most common types of anxiety disorder, and around 13 percent of the general population will experience symptoms of social anxiety disorder at one point in time. When an individual is suffering from social anxiety disorder, he or she constantly worries about how he or she is being perceived by other people. There is an irrational fear of being viewed negatively or judged, and of being embarrassed and humiliated. Social anxiety disorder differs from shyness because of the persistence and severity of the symptoms. Symptoms, which are both physical and emotional, include trembling, excessive sweating, a racing heart, extreme nervousness in situations where the individual does not know the other people, a strong fear of being evaluated, feeling anxious about being humiliated, fearing others will see that one is anxious, and fearing and dreading events that have been planned in advance.

SPECIFIC PHOBIAS

This type of anxiety disorder is when an individual has a strong and irrational fear of a particular object or situation. There are four major types of specific phobias, and many people will have multiple phobias within the same category—though an individual can also have phobias in multiple categories. The four major types are: situational, medical, natural environment, and animal-related.

No matter the category of phobia, when individuals have specific phobias, they exhibit similar symptoms. These include:

- Experiencing severe feelings of terror, panic, or dread when encountering the object the individual fears.
- Experiencing symptoms similar to a panic attack, including becoming short of breath, sweating profusely, becoming dizzy, and feeling numb.
- An individual will go out of his or her way to avoid the object he or she fears so much so that it affects his or her daily life and routine.
- The individual obsessively thinks about the next situation where he or she will encounter the feared object and creates scenarios in his or her head where coming into contact with the object is unavoidable.

GENERALIZED ANXIETY DISORDER

This is the most common type of anxiety disorder, where an individual experiences constant fear and tension regarding a matter or object without any reason for feeling this way. Worries seem as if they move from one subject matter to another, and symptoms are varied, but can include irritability, fatigue, difficulty focusing, restlessness, and sleep-related issues. Other physical symptoms that may arise include nausea, diarrhea, headaches, and tense muscles, particularly in the neck, shoulders, and back.

MARY AINSWORTH AND STRANGE SITUATIONS

Differing approaches to attachment

While psychologist John Bowlby claimed that when it came to attachment, it was all or nothing for a child, psychologist Mary Ainsworth took a different approach to the subject, believing that there were notable differences among individuals when it came to the quality of attachment.

Because one- to two-year-olds do not have the same capabilities as adults of expressing attachment, Ainsworth created an assessment technique known as the Strange Situation Classification (SSC) to understand individual differences in attachment, in 1970.

THE STRANGE SITUATION PROCEDURE

Ainsworth used around 100 middle-class families for her study, and all of the infants were between the ages of twelve to eighteen months old. To conduct her experiment, Ainsworth used a small room with one-way glass so she would be able to observe the infants' behavior. Seven experiments or "episodes," each lasting three minutes in length, were then conducted. Each episode was created to emphasize a particular behavior. The observers recorded their findings every fifteen seconds, and intensity of behavior was judged on a scale of 1 to 7.

EXPERMIENT

CONDUCTING THE EXPERIMENT

1. In the first stage of the experiment, the mother and infant are left to spend time alone in the room so that the infant can get used to the new environment.
2. Once the infant has adjusted to the new environment, a stranger enters the room and joins the parent and infant.

3. At this point, the mother departs, leaving the infant alone with the stranger.
4. The mother comes back into the room and the stranger leaves.
5. The mother then leaves the room as well, leaving the infant by him or herself.
6. The stranger then comes back into the room.
7. The mother then comes back into the room again, and the stranger leaves.

Ainsworth recorded the intensity of four different types of observed behaviors on a scale of 1 to 7. These types of behaviors included separation anxiety (a feeling of uneasiness from the infant when the mother left), the infant's eagerness to explore, stranger anxiety (how the infant responded when the stranger was present), and reunion behavior (the way the infant behaved when the mother returned). From this experiment, Ainsworth identified and named three separate attachment styles in the infants: secure, avoidant, and resistant.

SECURE ATTACHMENT

Children that are securely attached are confident that their mother, or attachment figure (AF), has the availability to meet their needs. The AF is sought out during times of trouble or distress, and is also used by the infant as a safe base so that the infant can then explore the environment. Ainsworth found that most children in her study were securely attached. When securely attached infants are upset, the AF can easily calm them. An infant will develop a secure attachment to the AF when the AF is perceptive to the child's signals and responds to the child's needs in an appropriate manner. Overall, Ainsworth found that 70 percent of the infants exhibited secure attachment, with common behaviors:

- In terms of separation anxiety, the child became distressed once the mother left the room.

- In terms of exploring his or her environment, Ainsworth concluded that the infant used the mother as a safe base.
- In terms of stranger anxiety, the infant was friendly to the stranger when the mother was in the room. When the mother was not present, however, the infant was avoidant of the stranger.
- In terms of reunion behavior, the infant became happier and more positive once the mother came back into the room.

INSECURE AVOIDANCE

Insecure avoidant children are more independent, and will not rely on the presence of their AF when investigating their environment. The infant's independence is not only physical, but also emotional; and when under stress, the child will not seek out the AF for help. The AF is insensitive, will not help when the infant is facing a hard task, will reject the infant's needs, and will be unavailable when the child is under emotional distress. Overall, Ainsworth found that 15 percent of the infants exhibited insecure avoidance:

- In terms of separation anxiety, the infants did not show any signs of distress when the mother left the room.
- In terms of stranger anxiety, the infant was fine with the stranger being in the room and acted normally.
- In terms of reunion behavior, as the mother came back into the room, the infant showed very little interest.
- Ainsworth found that both mother and stranger could comfort the infant equally.

INSECURE RESISTANCE

Insecure resistance is when the infant is hesitant or ambivalent toward the AF. Children showing signs of insecure resistance will reject the AF if the AF tries to engage and interact with the child. However, at other times, the child will behave in a clingy and dependent way. In this type of attachment, the child does not derive a sense of security from the AF; and as a result, the infant will find it difficult to move away from the AF to explore his or her environment. When a child exhibiting insecure resistance becomes upset or distressed, he or she is not comforted by the presence and contact of the AF, and will be difficult to calm. Overall, Ainsworth found that 15 percent of the infants exhibited insecure resistance.

- In terms of separation anxiety, the infants became extremely distressed once the mother left the room.
- In terms of stranger anxiety, the infant appeared to be afraid of the stranger and avoided the stranger.
- In terms of reunion behavior, when the mother entered the room again, the infant approached her but did not make contact with her, and would sometimes even push the mother away.

- Ainsworth found that infants with insecure resistance would explore less and cry more often than infants with secure attachment or insecure avoidance.

Later experiments replicating Ainsworth's Strange Situation experiment have given consistent results that match Ainsworth's, and it has become an accepted methodology in terms of measuring attachment. Ainsworth's findings have fallen under criticism, however, for only measuring attachment specific to the relationship between mother and infant. A child may have a completely different attachment style with his or her father, grandmother, grandfather, or other caretaker. Research has also shown that children may actually express different attachment behaviors at different times based on the circumstance.

MOOD DISORDERS

When emotions take over

Mood disorders are when disturbances in an individual's emotional state are so extreme that they affect his or her thinking processes, social relationships, and behavior. These tend to be episodic, meaning the symptoms will come and go. There are two major types of mood disorders that can be broken down into several sub-types. They are depressive disorder and bipolar disorder.

DEPRESSIVE DISORDERS

To be diagnosed with major depression, an individual has to experience a major depressive episode at least once. Major depressive episodes last for a period of two weeks or longer, and the individual will suffer from some, if not all, of the following symptoms:

- An overwhelming and consistent feeling of sadness or irritability
- Feeling guilty or worthless
- A loss of interest in doing anything, even previously enjoyable activities, and a lack of interest in being social
- Having very low energy
- Being unable to focus or make decisions
- Experiencing a change in eating patterns, either not eating well or eating too much
- Experiencing a change in sleeping patterns, either not being able to sleep or sleeping too much
- Experiencing recurrent thoughts of suicide or death

Interestingly enough, individuals that are extremely depressed will usually not commit suicide because during their major depressive episode, they feel too apathetic and unmotivated to create a suicide plan and follow through with it. Instead, it is during the recovery process, when the individual has more energy, that suicide becomes more prevalent. More women suffer from major depression than men. While more women also attempt suicide than men, men are more successful with following through with their suicide than women. In addition to major depression, there are several other types of depression that share these symptoms:

Dysthymia disorder

If a person experiences major depression symptoms for at least two years, then they have what is known as dysthymia disorder. It should be noted that people who suffer from this do not experience depressive symptoms at all times. There are moments when they do feel completely normal.

Seasonal affective disorder

Appropriately referred to as SAD, seasonal affective disorder is when a person suffers from symptoms of depression because of the time of the year. The majority of people who experience the condition do so in the wintertime.

Psychotic major depression

This is when an individual suffers from symptoms of major depression and also has hallucinations and delusions.

Postpartum depression

Postpartum depression occurs when a woman experiences depression following childbirth. This may be due to shifts in hormone levels, a lack of sleep, bodily changes, and changes in the woman's social or work relationships.

Atypical depression

This is a type of depression where an individual has many characteristics of major depression, but not enough symptoms to truly be classified as major depression. Symptoms in atypical depression usually include a gain in weight and increase in appetite, excessive sleeping or always feeling tired, and feeling very sensitive to any type of rejection.

Catatonic depression

This is a very rare type of depressive disorder where a person will become motionless for an extended period of time, or move in a violent or strange manner. People who suffer from catatonic depression will sometimes decide not to speak, or may even imitate the actions or speaking pattern of another individual.

Melancholic depression

This type of depression is characterized by losing interest and pleasure in many, if not all, activities. Individuals also find it very difficult to react positively when something good happens. Symptoms are generally worse in the morning, and early morning awakening can occur, where an individual wakes up on his or her own at least two hours too early without an external source causing the person to wake. Individuals suffering from melancholic depression also experience a very strong sadness that is obvious because of how different the person seems.

BIPOLAR DISORDERS

When an individual suffers from a bipolar disorder—once referred to as manic-depressive illness—they experience extreme mood swings between depression and mania. The symptoms of mania include:

- Feeling irritable
- Being extremely energetic
- Feeling high
- Feeling grandiose and having a very large self-esteem
- Feeling agitated
- Speaking in a fast manner
- Not needing to sleep as much or seemingly at all
- Having more interest in doing activities that bring pleasure, even if that means these activities can have harmful consequences
- Being impulsive
- Possibly having paranoia, delusions, and hallucinations

There are several types of bipolar disorder. These include:

Bipolar I Disorder

In bipolar I disorder, manic episodes or manic and depressive episodes last for at least seven days, or an individual will have such a strong manic episode that hospitalization is required. When people suffer from bipolar I disorder, they will generally also have depressive episodes that last for two weeks or longer.

Bipolar II Disorder

This is a milder type of bipolar disorder where episodes of hypomania and depression are not as severe.

Bipolar Disorder Not Otherwise Specified (BP-NOS)

This is when an individual suffers from symptoms of bipolar disorder—exhibiting symptoms that clearly stray from how the individual normally behaves—but does not meet the criteria needed to be diagnosed as having bipolar I or bipolar II. Symptoms in BP-NOS may last for too short an amount of time, or the individual may have too few symptoms.

Cyclothymia

This is a less severe type of bipolar disorder. While a person with cyclothymia will experience the same symptoms of bipolar I disorder, they will never be in a total manic state or have a major depressive episode. In order to be diagnosed as having cyclothymia, an individual must have these symptoms for at least two years.

LEV VYGOTSKY (1896–1934)

The importance of social interaction

Lev Vygotsky was born on November 17th, 1896, in a part of the Russian Empire known as Orsha, which is in present-day Belarus. Vygotsky actually graduated from the University of Moscow with a law degree in 1917, and his interest in psychology led him to attend the Institute of Psychology in Moscow, in 1924.

Vygotsky is most known for his work relating to education and childhood development, and his influence in cognitive development can still be seen to this day. Vygotsky believed that social interaction played a key role in cognitive development, and that people made meaning out of things through the lens of society and community. While Vygotsky lived at the same time as Freud, Skinner, Piaget, and Pavlov, the Communist party that ruled Russia at the time criticized his work, and most of his writings didn't get to reach the Western world until much later, in 1962, when Cold War tensions had begun to cease.

On June 11th, 1934, Vygotsky contracted tuberculosis and died. He was only thirty-eight years old. In his ten years working as a psychologist, Vygotsky published six books. His most important works were on his social development theory, which included his concept of the zone of proximal development and his work with language.

VYGOTSKY'S SOCIAL DEVELOPMENT THEORY

Greatly influenced by the work of Jean Piaget, Vygotsky believed that the human mind develops from the interactions between people and society. He hypothesized that certain tools from culture, like speech and the ability to write, were created so that people could interact with their social environment. According to Vygotsky, children will first develop these tools for social functions as a way to communicate to others what they need. But when these tools become internalized, the result is higher thinking skills.

Vygotsky placed an emphasis on social interaction in childhood, and claimed that children are constantly and gradually learning from their parents and teachers, but that this learning can be different depending on the culture. Furthermore, Vygotsky believed that not only did society have an impact on people, but that people also had an impact on society. Vygotsky's social development theory can be broken down into three major themes:

1. First, social development plays a key role in the development of cognitive processes. While Jean Piaget claimed that development had to come before learning, Vygotsky argued that social learning came before development of cognitive processes. He stated that first a development appears to

a child on a social level between people—known as the interpsychological—and then the child takes the information in on a more personal and individual level —called intrapsychological.

2. Second, Vygotsky described any person with a higher level of understanding than the learning individual as the More Knowledgeable Other (MKO). While the MKO can literally be anyone—a peer, someone younger, or even a computer—most of the time, MKOs are thought of as being teachers, adults, or a coach.
3. The final major theme in Vygotsky's social development theory is his "Zone of Proximal Development," or ZPD. According to Vygotsky, this is the distance between the ability of the person that is learning under the guidance of another person and the ability of the individual to solve the problem on his or her own. It is in this "zone" that learning occurs.

The Role of Language According to Vygotsky

Vygotsky believed language played two very important roles with regards to cognitive development. Language is the main method that adults use to transmit information to children, and through language, external experiences are converted into internal processes. Therefore, language is a powerful tool when it comes to adapting intellect. According to Vygotsky, language is created by social interaction with the purpose of communicating with one another. However, later on, language then becomes an "inner speech," which is the thoughts of a person. Therefore, language creates thoughts.

THE INFLUENCE OF VYGOTSKY

Today, a teaching method known as "reciprocal teaching" is based off of Vygotsky's theories. This teaching method focuses on improving children's abilities to acquire and learn information from text.

During reciprocal teaching, instead of having a teacher simply lecture at students, students and the teacher work together when learning and practicing, and go over key ideas such as how to summarize, how to question, how to clarify, and how to predict with one another. As time progresses, the teacher's role begins to decrease more and more. This not only ensures that the students are more active in the learning process, but also turns the relationship between student and teacher into one that is reciprocal, because as the roles shift, the teacher also needs the student to help create meaning. Reciprocal teaching is just one example of how important Lev Vygotsky's work was. His contributions and ideas related to developmental and educational psychology were groundbreaking, and because he was hidden from the Western world until 1962, his influence continues to grow to this day.

SOMATOFORM DISORDERS

Feeling the pain but not knowing why

Somatoform disorders are mental illnesses where an individual suffers from actual physical symptoms that cannot be explained by a physical medical condition. For something to be diagnosed as a somatoform disorder, it must adhere to certain criteria:

1. The physical symptoms can't be the result of a medical condition, use of drugs, or from another mental illness.
2. The diagnosis cannot be malingering (when a patient exhibits physical symptoms so that they can have an external gain, often in the form of money) or a factitious disorder (where an individual exhibits physical symptoms for an internal gain, like

wanting others to feel bad for them).

3. The symptoms have to greatly impair the functioning of the individual's occupational, social, and daily life.

There are seven types of somatoform disorders. They are:

Somatization Disorder (otherwise known as Briquet's syndrome)

Somatization disorder generally presents itself before the age of thirty, and is found in more women than men. Symptoms include pain in at least four distinct areas of the body, problems with the reproductive system, like erectile dysfunction or a lack of interest in sex, gastrointestinal problems including diarrhea and vomiting, and pseudoneurological symptoms like blindness or fainting.

Undifferentiated Somatoform Disorder

This is a type of somatization disorder where an individual has only one of the symptoms from somatization disorder, and the patient experiences it for a period of at least six months.

Conversion Disorder

Symptoms of conversion disorder generally occur after an individual has experienced a stressful or traumatic event, and the condition typically affects the voluntary motor and sensory functions. Common symptoms include paralysis, numbness, blindness, and being unable to speak. For example, if a man is riding a horse and falls off of it, he may experience leg paralysis following the fall, even though in all reality his leg is completely fine and unharmed. Many believe that the physical symptoms of conversion disorder are the person's attempt to resolve the conflict inside of him or her.

Pain Disorder

A person suffering from pain disorder will experience chronic and severe pain that could last for several months. Unlike malingering, where an individual will fake the sensation of pain, when a person suffers from pain disorder, they are in an extremely large amount of pain, which has a dramatic effect on the individual's daily life.

Hypochondriasis

Hypochondriasis, or hypochondria, is when an individual is preoccupied with the fear of having a very serious disease. By misinterpreting their own symptoms, people will determine that their symptoms are much more serious than they actually are. Even after being seen and evaluated by a doctor, the preoccupation with and belief in the symptoms will continue, or go away for a short time and then come right back. Unlike malingering, people that suffer from hypochondriasis are not simply making symptoms up. Instead, these people cannot control their feelings and are convinced that any type of symptom is a sign of a serious illness. Individuals can be said to have hypochondriasis when they have been exhibiting this type of behavior for at least six months and their symptoms cannot be explained by other conditions, like panic disorder, obsessive-compulsive disorder, or generalized anxiety disorder.

Body Dysmorphic Disorder

When a person suffers from body dysmorphic disorder, they become obsessive over a deformity or physical imperfection that may exist, or may not exist at all. This type of somatoform disorder features a preoccupation with physical defects that are either trivial or completely nonexistent, and this obsession creates distress socially, occupationally, and throughout the individual's daily life. An example of body dysmorphic disorder could be a woman who always wears gloves because she has a small scar on one of her hands. The woman fixates and obsesses over something very trivial. In order to classify a somatoform disorder as a body dysmorphic disorder, none of the symptoms can be explained by other disorders. For example, when a person is concerned about his or her weight, this is usually the result of an eating disorder instead of body dysmorphic disorder.

Somatoform Disorder Not Otherwise Specified (NOS)

When a person suffers from symptoms characteristic of a somatoform disorder, but does not meet the conditions related to any one specific disorder.

CONTRIBUTING FACTORS OF SOMATOFORM DISORDERS

Researchers believe that cognitive and personality factors play a large role in the development of somatoform disorders.

Cognitive Factors

The cognitive factors that researchers believe contribute to the development of a somatoform disorder include:

- Having a distorted notion of what good health is, and therefore expecting a healthy person to never have discomfort or ever have any symptoms
- Focusing too much on bodily sensations
- Coming to very extreme conclusions when experiencing only

minor symptoms

Personality Factors

Many believe that people with histrionic personality traits have a greater chance of developing a somatoform disorder. These people behave in particular ways to get the attention of others, are very emotional and dramatic, are very open to suggestion, and are self-focused. The combination of these factors seems to increase the likelihood of falling victim to a self-generated somatoform disorder.

FALSE CONSENSUS AND UNIQUENESS EFFECTS

Everything I do, you do ... right?

The false consensus effect is the phenomenon that occurs among people where the tendency exists to think that our opinions and beliefs are the common opinions and beliefs amongst everyone else. Similarly, the false uniqueness effect is a phenomenon wherein people underestimate just how common their abilities and desirable attributes really are. The false consensus effect and the false uniqueness effect are examples of cognitive biases, which are flaws in judgment caused by the mind so that the brain can process information at a faster rate.

LEE ROSS'S FALSE CONSENSUS EFFECT EXPERIMENTS

While there is very little experimental evidence that shows the false uniqueness effect in action, there has been more substantial work with regards to the false consensus effect. In 1977, Stanford University professor Lee Ross created a series of experiments to look at how the false consensus effect works.

Ross's First Study

In his first experiment, Ross began by having a group of participants read about situations that involved some type of conflict. He then gave the group of people two ways to respond to the situation, and asked them to do three things:

1. Guess the option that the other people in the group would choose
2. Say the option that they would choose themselves
3. Describe the qualities and characteristics of the type of person that would choose the first option and the second option

The results from this experiment showed that the majority of the subjects believed others would choose the same option as them, no matter which option they chose, thus validating the false consensus effect.

Interestingly, when responding to the third part of the experiment, the qualities and personalities that the participants associated with those people that chose the option that wasn't their own were very extreme. To put it bluntly, they took the mindset of "if you don't agree with what I have to say, then you must be wrong."

Ross's Second Study

In Ross's second study, a new group of participants was asked if they would willingly walk around the college campus for thirty minutes while wearing a sandwich board that said, "Eat at Joe's." As a means of motivation, Ross told the test subjects that by the end of the experiment, the participants would learn something useful. He also informed them that they were free to say no if they wanted. Ross then asked the group of people the same questions as he did in the first study.

Sixty-two percent of the people who agreed to participate in the experiment believed that others would do the same, and only 33 percent of people who did not wear the sandwich board thought that other people would wear the sandwich board. Ross's second study confirmed the results from his first study; and much like the first study, the subjects made extreme predictions about what type of person would choose the answer they did not choose.

THE IMPACT OF ROSS'S EXPERIMENTS

Lee Ross was able to successfully prove the existence of the false consensus effect and show that people have the tendency to judge how everyone else should make their decisions based on how they, themselves, would make a decision. Ross also showed that if someone else makes a decision that the individual does not agree with or would not choose, then the individual tends to view that person in a negative light, and see him or her as unacceptable or defective.

PROVING FALSE UNIQUENESS

While there is very little empirical evidence for false uniqueness, in 1988, Jerry Suls, Choi K. Wan, and Glenn S. Sanders published an article looking into the phenomenon of false uniqueness with regards to how individuals perceive their own health-related behavior.

To conduct the study, the researchers used a group of college-aged men as their subjects. They first hypothesized that false consensus effect would occur where people would perceive their own healthy behaviors (such as exercising) to be common among those that also performed healthy behavior. They then hypothesized that those people who performed in ways that were undesirable (like not exercising) would overestimate the number of people behaving the way they behaved, and that those who behaved in a desirable way (those that exercised) would underestimate the amount of people behaving in this way.

The results of their experiment found strong evidence supporting the first two hypotheses, and some evidence suggesting the third hypothesis to be true. It is believed that the people who displayed undesirable behavior resist any sort of intervention and don't practice healthy behavior by overestimating the consensus of their behavior, and that some may even believe there are few health risks involved for them. While this does show some proof of the false uniqueness effect, further research is needed.

The bias created by false consensus effect can have a very dramatic impact on society and has very real implications. One of the most startling examples of the false consensus effect can be seen in the negative viewpoints found in fundamentalists and political radicals. While these people do not necessarily think that most people have their radical viewpoints and beliefs, they do overestimate the number of those that do, which further twists their perceptions of the world around them.

STRESS

The science behind the pressure

Stress is when a physiological response is elicited from external stimuli. The stimuli can be both psychological and physiological, and stress can be long-term or short-term. Despite the way we speak about it, stress is not simply a feeling; it can actually affect a person's biological and psychological state. When we think of stress, we tend to think of it as being equivalent to worry, but stress is much more than that, and it does not always have to be bad. There are actually two types of stress: distress and eustress, which occur from negative and positive events, respectively.

Clinical Definitions

DISTRESS: Stress that occurs from negative events. For example, the stress that occurs from experiencing the death of a loved one, getting hurt, or losing a job.

EUSTRESS: Stress that occurs from positive events. For example, the stress that occurs when watching a scary movie, going on a roller coaster, or getting a job promotion.

THE FIGHT OR FLIGHT RESPONSE

In the 1920s, American physiologist Walter Cannon described a theory about how animals handle stress based on behavior. He called this theory the fight or flight response, otherwise known as acute stress.

According to Cannon, when an animal is under intense stress (even if the stress is not real), a psychological and physiological reaction is triggered. There will be a sudden release of chemicals including adrenaline, norepinephrine, and cortisol in the body. This will create an increase in heart rate, an increase in breathing, a tightening of the muscles, and a constricting of blood vessels, resulting in the energy necessary to react by either fighting or fleeing. This involuntary response is regulated by three bodily systems: the immune system, the endocrine system, and the central nervous system.

HANS SELYE'S EXPERIMENTS WITH RATS

The effect that stress can have on the body was first described by Hungarian scientist Hans Selye, in 1936. Selye theorized that chronic stress creates long-term chemical changes in the body, and therefore, stress could be a prominent cause of diseases.

Selye had actually stumbled upon this conclusion while working with rats as an assistant at McGill University's biochemistry department. He had been working on an experiment that involved injecting rats with ovarian extract, hoping to discover a reaction that would lead to a new type of sex hormone.

The rats did react: their spleens, thymuses, lymph nodes, and adrenal cortexes enlarged, and they had deep bleeding ulcers in their duodenums and stomach linings. As Selye adjusted the amount of extract, these reactions would increase and decrease accordingly. Hans Selye was under the impression that he had discovered a new hormone. However, he then tried the experiment with placental extract and pituitary extract. To his surprise, the rats had the exact same responses. Still under the impression that this was a new hormone he was dealing with, Selye then tried the experiment once more with the extracts of several organs, including the kidney and spleen. The same reactions occurred every single time. Confused by these results, Selye tried one last thing: he injected a type of formaldehyde into the rats. This too brought about the same results.

HANS SELYE'S GENERAL ADAPTATION SYNDROME

Considering his experiments with the rats to be a failure (because, after all, no new hormone was discovered), Hans Selye began looking into other possible causes for the symptoms he had discovered. A few years later, he recalled an experience he had had while studying as a young medical student in Prague. Patients would come in complaining of intestinal issues, as well as general aches and pains. Upon further examination, the patients would also end up having a fever, an enlarged liver or spleen, a skin rash, and inflamed tonsils. It wasn't until later on that diagnosable symptoms related to particular illnesses began to appear.

Selye also became intrigued by the notion that doctors always ordered patients to perform certain treatments no matter what they were suffering from—treatments including rest, eating easily digestible food, and avoiding rooms that varied in temperature.

From his lab work with the rats and his memories of medical school, Hans Selye identified what he referred to as the general adaptation syndrome, which describes the body's reactions to stress. According to Selye, the general adaptation syndrome can be broken down into three stages:

1. **Alarm Reaction:** This is when homeostasis is disturbed by a stressor or external stimulus and the body first notices this stimulus. It is in this first stage that Cannon's fight or flight response comes into effect and hormones are released to provide the individual with enough energy to handle the situation at hand.

   If the energy that is released from the fight or flight response continually remains unused through a lack of physical activity, it can actually have harmful effects on the body. Too much of the hormone cortisol, for example, can damage muscle tissue and cells, and can even lead to gastric ulcers, high blood sugar levels, and stroke. If there is too much adrenaline in the body, blood vessels of the brain and heart can be damaged, and this will increase the risk of suffering from a stroke or heart attack.

2. **Adaptation:** This is when the body begins to counteract the external stimulus and restore homeostasis through recovery, renewal, and repair. This process is known as resistance, and it occurs almost immediately after the beginning of the alarm phase, and will continue until the stressful condition desists. Should a stressful condition continue, the body will remain in its state of arousal.

   A person will begin to face problems when this process begins repeating too frequently, leaving little to no time for recovery to set in. If this occurs, the individual will move into the next stage.

3. **Exhaustion:** This is when the body has been depleted of the energy, both physical and psychological, required to fight off

> the stressor. This is particularly true for chronic stressors, because when fighting short-term stress, a person may not be entirely depleted of his or her energy. With the energy lost, the individual can no longer resist the stressor.

As a result, stress levels go up and remain high. The individual may experience adrenal fatigue, burnout, maladaptation, overload, or dysfunction. The result of chronic stress on the body and mind is also quite striking. Nerve cells of organs and tissues can become damaged, memory and thinking can become impaired, and a person will be more likely to have anxiety or depression. High levels of stress can also contribute to rheumatoid arthritis, high blood pressure, and heart disease.

SELF-DISCREPANCY THEORY

The impact of fulfillment (or lack thereof)

From 1987 to 1999, psychologist Edward Tory Higgins created a concept that attempted to explain the source of all dejection and anxiety; he called it the self-discrepancy theory. According to Higgins's theory, an individual will experience dejection when he or she feels his or her hopes and ambitions have not been fulfilled, and an individual will experience anxiety when he or she feels as if a duty or obligation of his or hers has not been fulfilled.

The self-discrepancy theory states that throughout an individual's life, he or she will realize that achieving goals and aspirations can lead to certain secure rewards, like approval and love. The aspirations and achievements merge to create a set of principles, and these form a guide of the ideal self. When a person feels as if he or she may not be capable of achieving one of these goals, he or she gradually begins to anticipate the loss of the rewards; as a result, dejection, depression, and disappointment occur.

The self-discrepancy theory also states that throughout an individual's life, he or she will learn to fulfill obligations and duties in order to prevent punishment and unfavorable results. As time progresses, these experiences will create an abstract set of principles for the individual that will act as a guide, and if he or she feels the obligations and duties within this guide have not been fulfilled, he or she will experience feelings or a sense of punishment. This feeling of punishment comes across as anxiety and agitation.

EVIDENCE OF THE SELF-DISCREPANCY THEORY

In 1997, Edward Tory Higgins and fellow researchers conducted an experiment in an attempt to prove the self-discrepancy theory.

The experiment first had participants list any traits that they wished they had, and then list any traits that they felt they should have. These were known as the "ideal" and "ought" characteristics. Participants then described the amount of these traits that they already were exhibiting. In the final step of the experiment, the amount of emotions experienced were assessed by participants using a four-point scale.

The results of the experiment were consistent with the ideas put forth by the self-discrepancy theory. Those individuals that felt their ideals were not fulfilled—referred to as an actual-ideal discrepancy—had a higher rate of dejection, and those individuals that were unsatisfied with their oughts—referred to as actual-ought discrepancy—had a higher rate of agitation.

COMPLICATIONS

There are several complicating factors to the self-discrepancy theory, however. The emotions that are the result of self-discrepancies are dependent upon whether or not the person chose those particular aspirations by themselves. Higgins claimed that failing to achieve goals that were imposed by another individual will result in feelings of embarrassment and shame, not disappointment or dejection. Similarly, failing to fulfill obligations that were imposed by another person created feelings of resentment.

In 1998, a study was conducted that challenged the self-discrepancy theory by proving that any type of discrepancy led to feelings of shame, and that instead of anxiety, it was actually feelings of depression that came from actual-ideal and actual-ought discrepancies. This study was one of several that attempted to establish alternatives to Higgins's self-discrepancy model. Several of the proposed alternatives follow here.

Money on the Mind

For many, the discrepancy between existing wealth, status, and possessions and desired wealth, status, and possessions is a constant source of dejection and agitation. While it may be common to strive to gain more and increase traits, studies have shown that this does not significantly improve well-being, and may actually do the opposite. In several studies, it was commonly found that while people desired more money than they currently had, it had no bearing on their emotions and satisfaction with life, and the discrepancies these people had in terms of how much money they had and how much money they wanted was inversely related to their well-being (emotions and satisfaction).

MULTIPLE DISCREPANCIES

In 1985, Alex Michalos created the multiple discrepancy theory, which claimed that people may feel dissatisfied or unhappy from three things: if the resources acquired throughout their life are not the same as, or more than, the resources acquired by key figures in their life (known as a social comparison discrepancy); if people had access to more resources at one point in time but no longer have the same access (known as past comparison discrepancy); and if people have not acquired resources they desired (known as desire discrepancy, similar to the idea found in the self-discrepancy theory).

THE UNDESIRED SELF

Rather than focusing on ideals, some researchers believe that discrepancies that come from the *undesired* self play a more important role with regards to mood and satisfaction. In a 1987 study conducted by Rutgers University professor Daniel M. Ogilvie, an assessment of the actual selves, ideal selves, and undesired selves was taken. In order to measure the undesired self, participants had to describe what they were like at their worst. The study found that discrepancies between the actual self and the undesired self were very strongly associated with satisfaction, while discrepancies between the actual self and ideal self were not as strongly associated with satisfaction.

The theory behind these results is that the undesired self is more grounded in reality, while the ideal self is too vague of a concept because it is not rooted by any real experiences.

ESCAPE THEORY

Escape theory claims that when a person feels important standards are unattainable, he or she will develop a large self-discrepancy, and the result will be a strong impulse to escape from the reality of oneself. The desire to escape can show itself as behaviors like excessive sleeping, use of drugs, and suicidal tendencies.

According to escape theory, there are a number of phases that occur prior to a suicide attempt:

1. A person will feel a sense of disappointment or failure because he or she has become aware of the discrepancy between the standards he or she expects to accomplish and him or herself.

2. The person will then attribute the failure to him or herself instead of attributing it to the transient situations.
3. The person then becomes extremely aware of him or herself, and begins to constantly evaluate his or her own behavior. This state of awareness heightens the individual's negative feelings about him or herself.
4. Cognitive deconstruction occurs, where the person rejects any previous perspectives, avoids goals, thinks in concrete terms, and rejects meaning in anything. From this deconstructed state, drastic measures, irrational behavior, and negative emotions seem acceptable and amplified.

Suicide then becomes the ultimate escape for the individual. Such a downward spiral shows the innate power of these types of discrepancies, whether between the real self and the ideal self, or between the real self and the undesired self.

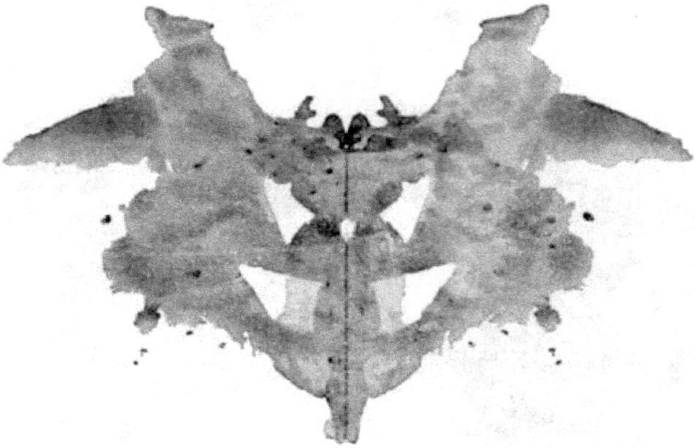

THE FIRST RORSCHACH BLOT

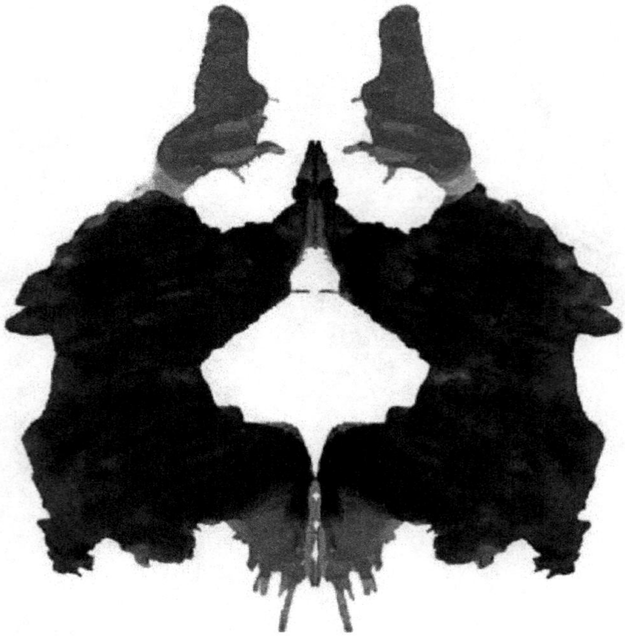

THE SECOND RORSCHACH BLOT

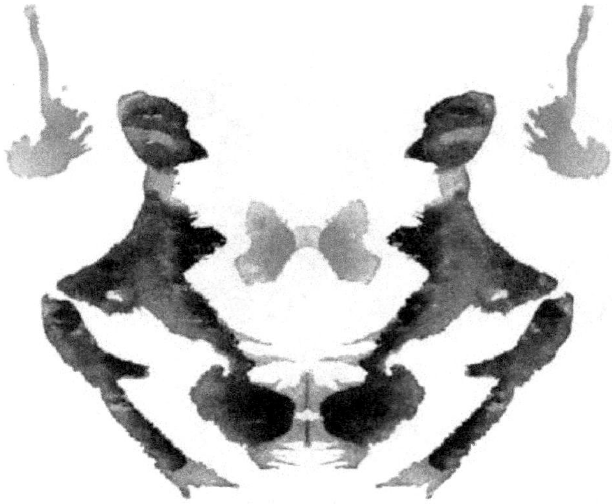

THE THIRD RORSCHACH BLOT

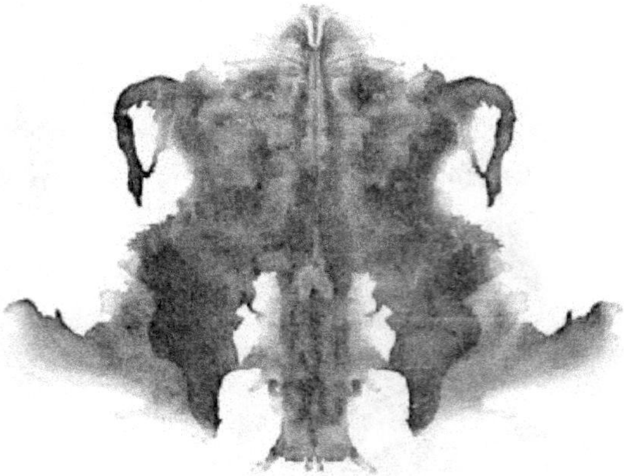

THE FOURTH RORSCHACH BLOT

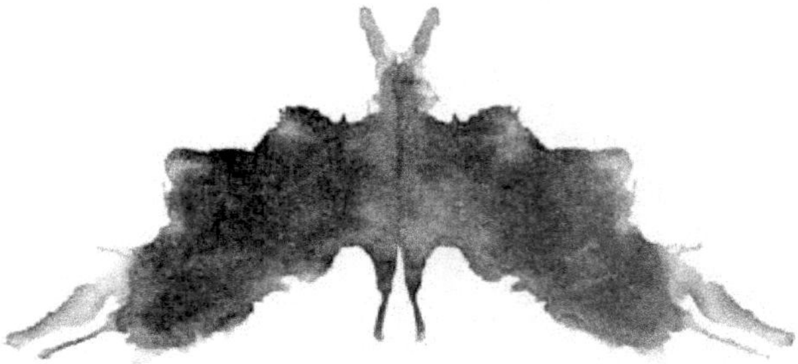

THE FIFTH RORSCHACH BLOT

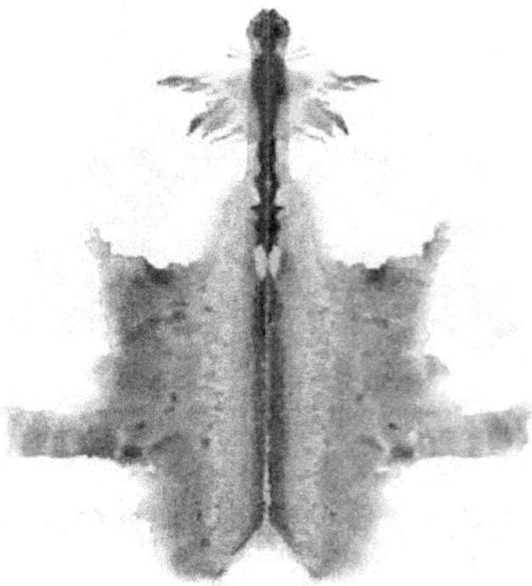

THE SIXTH RORSCHACH BLOT

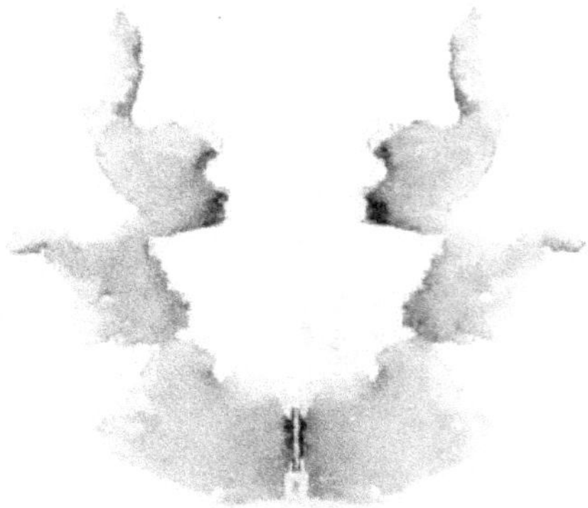

THE SEVENTH RORSCHACH BLOT

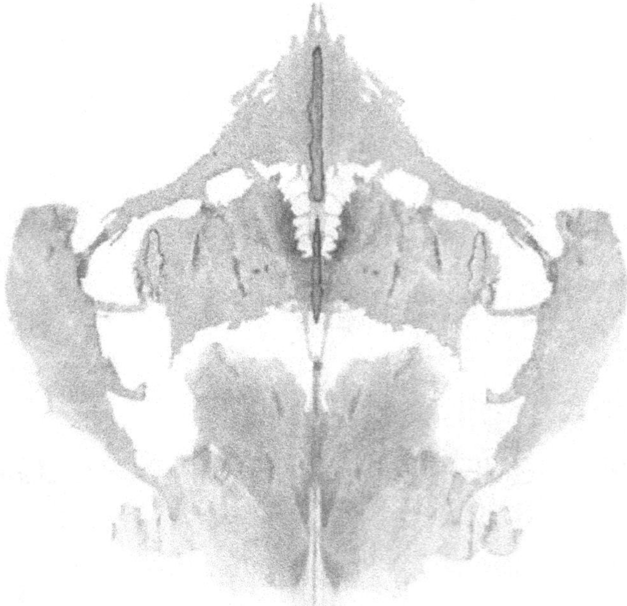

THE EIGHTH RORSCHACH BLOT

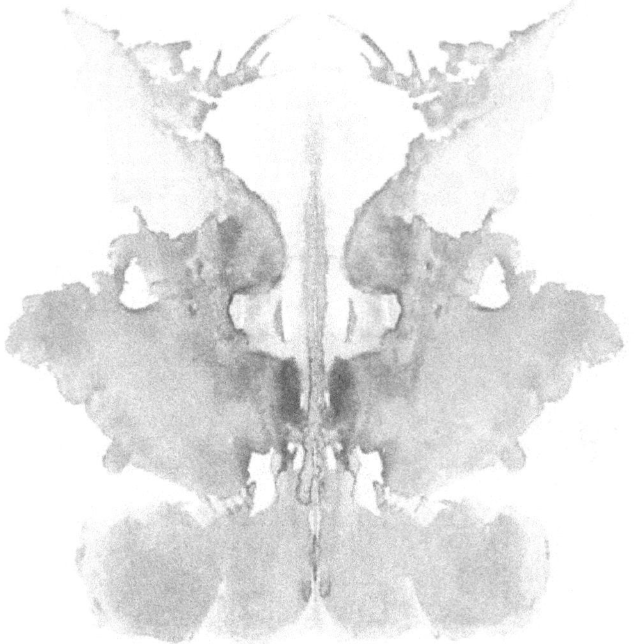

THE NINTH RORSCHACH BLOT

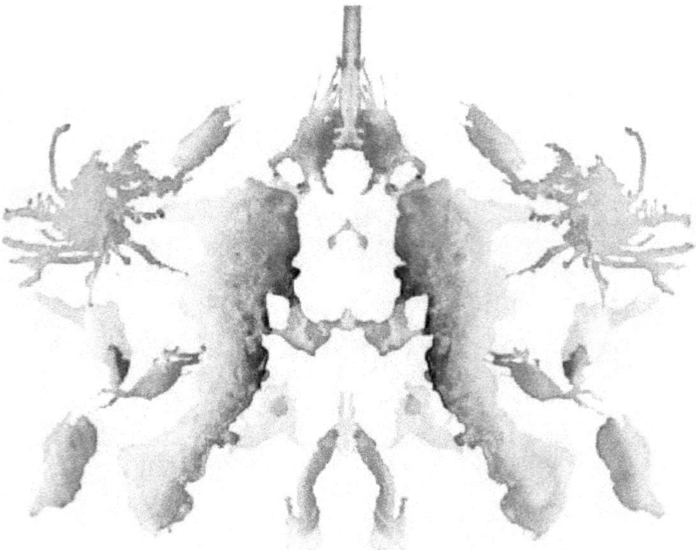

THE TENTH RORSCHACH BLOT

CPSIA information can be obtained
at www.ICGtesting.com
Printed in the USA
LVHW020009280423
745413LV00009B/165

9 781806 314133